T0270151

A SUMMER WITH PASCAL

A
SUMMER
WITH
PASCAL

ANTOINE COMPAGNON

Translated by CATHERINE PORTER

THE BELKNAP PRESS *of* HARVARD UNIVERSITY PRESS

Cambridge, Massachusetts & London, England

2024

First published as *Un été avec Pascal,* copyright © 2020 by Éditions des Équateurs /
Humensis / France Inter

Library of Congress Cataloging-in-Publication Data

Names: Compagnon, Antoine, 1950– author. | Porter, Catherine, 1941– translator.
Title: A summer with Pascal / Antoine Compagnon ; translated by Catherine Porter.
Other titles: Été avec Pascal. English
Description: Cambridge, Massachusetts ; London, England : The Belknap Press of
   Harvard University Press, 2024. | Translation of : Un été avec Pascal. | Includes
   bibliographical references.
Identifiers: LCCN 2023032382 | ISBN 9780674295414 (cloth)
Subjects: LCSH: Pascal, Blaise, 1623–1662.
Classification: LCC B1903 .C655 2024 | DDC 194—dc23/eng/20230811
LC record available at https://lccn.loc.gov/2023032382

Contents

Note on the Translation

*T*he work assembled by scholars under the title *Pensées* (literally, "Thoughts") is a collection of fragmentary passages from which Pascal intended to develop an apologia for the Christian religion. All translations from the *Pensées* in the current text are my own, as are translations from Pascal's *Œuvres complètes* and other texts where no translator is identified. The fragment numbers supplied for the *Pensées* are those found in *Les Provinciales, Pensées, et opuscules divers*, edited by Philippe Sellier and Gérard Ferreyrolles. The Works Cited section provides full documentation for all quoted material. The explanatory footnotes are my own.

I thank my husband, Philip Lewis, a scholar of seventeenth-century French literature, for his invaluable help in untangling the nuances of the language and thought of Pascal's day.

Preface

*A*fter Montaigne, who inaugurated the "A Summer with . . ." radio series on France Inter, how could I fail to take up, sooner or later, the writer who was his best reader? Pascal was Montaigne's most attentive disciple but also his most vigorous adversary. The *Pensées* grew out of an "Against Montaigne," just as *In Search of Lost Time* grew out of an "Against Sainte-Beuve" buried under Proust's novel.[1] "Montaigne is wrong" (454), Pascal proclaims, on almost all the subjects he touches on in his own *Pensées:* "He talks about himself too much" (534), "he thinks only about dying, in a spineless and nonchalant way, throughout the whole book" (559), his failings are "great," especially his "foolish project to picture himself!" (644). Montaigne turns up everywhere in the *Pensées,* for he was the model for the *honnêtes hommes*[2] whom Pascal is trying to convert. No thinker was more opposed

---

1. Shortly before beginning *In Search of Lost Time (À la recherche du temps perdu),* Marcel Proust had started to write an article, published only posthumously in 1954, that rejected mid-nineteenth-century French writer and literary critic Charles-Augustin Sainte-Beuve's idea that one cannot separate an author from their biography.

2. See Chapter 40 of the present book for a partial definition: "The honnête homme is first of all someone who is honorable, sociable, courteous, and polite." A gentleman, then, but one who manifests certain moral qualities, including generosity and altruism.

to Montaigne than Pascal, but the *Pensées* would be inconceivable without the *Essays*. The two writers form one of those inseparable pairs from whom French literature derives its glory.

To speak of Pascal is thus to approach one of the partners in the miraculous duo that founded our modernity, by which I mean the freedom to think. Both writers deal with everything and anything, free from all preconceived notions: humankind, society, the universe, power, faith, anguish, death, play. . . . And Pascal contradicts Montaigne, condemns his skepticism and his nonchalance, but he also occasionally connects with him, after some reflection. For example, their political choices are similar: they both mistrust reforms and fear disorder; enlightened conservatism brings them together.

For the summer with Montaigne, a few years ago, we improvised. I drafted my chronicle like a serial publication; I recorded it in short segments without knowing where I would go next. For Pascal, the series was well established, and more discipline was imposed: I was supposed to record the whole thing in one go. Proceeding by leaps and bounds no doubt served Montaigne better, but I was nevertheless apprehensive about the lost liberty that threatened to make the Pascal chronicle more pedantic; since the end would already have been written, I would know where I was going.

However, circumstances dictated otherwise. While I was plunging impatiently back into Pascal (my loyalty to whom goes back to the first university courses I taught some forty years ago), the health of a person dear to me took an irremediable turn for the worse. I spent my time with her, untangling the *Provincial*

Letters[3] and the *Pensées* at her bedside, taking notes, scribbling. She read a first batch of chronicles, made comments, suggested revisions. But the scheduled recordings had to be canceled. What followed, since she no longer had the strength to read, was my reading them to her in an "end-of-life house," a hospice. I'm pretty sure that the last chronicle to which she reacted with conviction was "The heart has its reasons." We had a discussion about the affinities between Pascal's reflections on the heart and contemporary thinking about the emotions, and I reworked my text in response. During the final days, I read two more to her, "What is the self?" and "Village queens and false windows," but I skipped certain passages in Pascal that I didn't want her to hear.

It seems outrageous to put it this way, but Pascal was useful to me—or even to us—as a distraction. I kept reciting a particular fragment of the *Pensées* that troubled me enormously: "This man so afflicted by the death of his wife and his only son, and so consumed by a serious dispute—how does it happen that he is not sad and looks so untouched by all those painful and worrying thoughts? There is no reason to be astonished by this: he has just been served a ball and has to pass it back to his companion" (453).

The ball I was running after and trying as hard as I could to send back was that thought itself. I was playing with Pascal, and the game distracted me; it helped me get through the days and the nights.

---

3. Pascal's *Provincial Letters* (*Lettres provinciales*), initially published under a pseudonym, contains a series of witty letters purportedly addressed to a friend in the provinces but also to Jesuit priests and scholars with whom the author is engaged in a fierce theological debate over divine grace and free will.

There is no shame in recognizing this, just one more paradox, a figure that is hardly in short supply in Pascal's reasoning. And indeed, such paradoxes are proof of the profound human truth and the terrible relevance of the *Pensées*. We argued over the heart and the mind up to her last breath, not to hide reality from ourselves, not to veil the truth, but because everything Pascal writes is so provocative that only death succeeds in shutting us up—the infinite silence.

The recordings, made under difficult conditions, required all the patience of producer Anne Weinfeld and of producer and performer Sophie Ferdiane, who successfully adjusted to a disrupted calendar and whom I thank here. I am also grateful to Laurence Bloch, Anne-Julie Bémont, and Olivier Frébourg, who renewed their confidence in me and wagered on uncertainty.

Thirty-five chronicles were broadcast on the radio, but I had decided to write forty, as I had done for Montaigne. Then, at the last minute, I wrote a forty-first, as a bonus. I leave the reader to guess which one.

A SUMMER WITH PASCAL

1

"That Terrifying Genius"

Ma nuit chez Maud, one of Éric Rohmer's "Moral Tales," takes place in Clermont-Ferrand. Pascal, who was born there, comes up a lot in the film, which was made more than fifty years ago, in 1969. At the beginning of the movie, Jean-Louis Trintignant, who plays a young Catholic engineer troubled by desire, is in a bookstore skimming through a volume of Pascal's complete works. Later, at Maud's place (Maud being the young woman with whom he'll spend the night), the conversation comes back to the author of the *Pensées.* Maud recalls the two or three things she knows about him, the kinds of things one recalls long after one's school days: she cites the thinking reed (145) and the two infinities (230). She could have added the wager (680), Cleopatra's nose (32, 79), Cromwell's bladder (622), or the "village queens" (486).[1] The *Pensées* includes a wealth of unforgettable

---

1. The numbers in parentheses refer to individual fragments in the *Pensées* according to the numbering system developed by Jean Mesnard and used by editors Philippe Sellier and Gérard Ferreyrolles in *Les Provinciales, Pensées, et opuscules divers.*

formulas and images. Pascal was one of the greatest virtuosos of the French language but first and foremost an incomparable mathematician and physicist and a peerless philosopher and theologian.

No one has better expressed the admiration that Pascal inspires in us and the legend that surrounds him than Chateaubriand, in *The Genius of Christianity* (p. 411):

> There was a genius who, at the age of twelve years, had with *bars* and *rings* created the mathematics; who, at sixteen, had composed the ablest treatise on conic sections that had appeared since the time of the ancients; who, at nineteen, reduced to a machine a science existing entirely in the understanding; who, at twenty-three, demonstrated the phenomena of the gravity of the air, and overthrew one of the great errors of ancient physics; who, at an age when the intellectual faculties scarcely begin to expand in others, having gone through the whole circle of human sciences, discovered their inanity, and turned all his thoughts toward religion; who, from that moment till his death (which happened in his thirty-ninth year) amid incessant bodily infirmities, fixed the language spoken by Bossuet and Racine, and furnished a model of the most perfect facetiousness as well as of the strongest reasoning; finally, who, in the short intervals of ease, resolved, unassisted, one of the profoundest problems of geometry, and scattered at random upon paper thoughts not less indicative of a superhuman than of a human mind. The name of this stupendous genius was BLAISE PASCAL.

Chateaubriand sees Pascal as a Romantic hero, a Promethean giant. He confuses him with his adversary or interlocutor in the

Pensées, the libertine: that is, the atheist or the agnostic in religious matters, the one whom Pascal is seeking to convert by confronting him with the frightfulness of his condition. Pascal is not that libertine. He has certainties—or he adopts an air of certainty, for faith does not protect against doubt; in contrast, we moderns think that the libertine's existential anguish is Pascal's own, and we identify with him. This is why the argument of the wager has remained so striking, along with some memorable notions that describe fallen humankind: diversion, cause of the effects, thought in the back of the mind, the intuitive mind. A number of striking sentences are burned into the brain of every French person: "The eternal silence of those infinite spaces frightens me" (233); "whoever wants to act the angel acts the beast" (557); "the heart has its reasons, which reason does not know" (680).

Pascal, for us, represents the person divided between science and faith, subjected to the tragedy of a hidden God, to the anguish of the human condition, and we neglect the fact that the *Pensées* offer the rudiments of an "Apology for the Christian Religion," even if Pascal never uses that wording.

In Proust's *The Way by Swann's,* Swann expresses his admiration for Pascal in a paradox:

> What I fault the newspapers for is that day after day they draw our attention to insignificant things whereas only three or four times in our lives do we read a book in which there is something really essential. Since we tear the band off the newspaper so feverishly every morning, they ought to change things and put into the newspaper, oh, I don't know, perhaps . . . Pascal's Pensées! . . .

And then, in the gilt-edged volume that we open only once in
ten years, . . . we would read that the Queen of Greece has gone
to Cannes or that the Princesse de Léon has given a costume ball.
This way, the proper proportions would be re-established. (29)

The *Pensées* are a masterpiece of French literature, but first of all
mixed-up fragments of an apologia whose drafting was interrupted
by illness and death. Would we find the work as seductive if Pascal
had finished it, if it had become a treatise without the dazzling form
of fireworks?

2

"Heel of a Shoe"

The *Pensées* are shot through with elliptical fragments that stop us in our tracks with their oddness. One example: "The parrot's beak, which it wipes even though it is clean" (139). Then the author says that this is a remark about automatic movements, about animal-machines as Descartes conceived of them: if the parrot had enough of a mind to reflect, he would not keep on wiping his beak when it was already clean. Now, certain people, perhaps even all of us, behave like animals, machines, automatons. For instance, a chatterer, "the doctor who talks for a quarter of an hour after having said everything, so full is he of the desire to speak" (483).

Automatisms are for Pascal a mark of human wretchedness. Here is another of these mysterious fragments from the *Pensées:* "Heel of a shoe. / Oh, how well crafted it is! Now, there's a skillful worker! How bold that soldier is! There is the source of our inclinations and our choice of situations. This person drinks too much! That person drinks too little! That is what makes people sober or drunks, soldiers, cowards, etc." (69).

"Heel of a shoe." This recurrent motif in the *Pensées* has haunted me for a long time. I find that image so striking that if I were writing my own memoirs, I would like to title them *Heel of a Shoe*.

The fragment illustrates the absurdity of our behaviors, the arbitrariness of our most important decisions, which we take lightly. We depend on chance; we base our essential life choices on whims and trivialities. One adopts one's trade not in response to a deep vocation but for anodyne, vain, empty reasons: its reputation, the expected compliments. A "well-crafted heel": this insignificant detail is the derisory illustration of our vanity, the pride that can be attached to one of the lowest-ranking trades under the Old Regime, that of the cobbler.

Pascal comes back to the subject frequently: "Trades / The sweetness of glory is so great that we love whatever object we attach to it, even death" (71).

So much for the vocation of men of war, stupidly seduced by the honor of a heroic death. Pascal classified this fragment, like "Heel of a shoe," in the group labeled "Vanity" in the *Pensées*. He classified his mass of fragments in 1658, outlining his "Apology" in twenty-seven ordered sheaves. The first ten developed an anthropology, or a picture of the human condition, and the seventeen that followed sketched out a theology, or a pathway toward God.

Part One: Wretchedness of man without God.
Part Two: Felicity of man with God.
    otherwise

Part One: That nature is corrupt, demonstrated by nature.

Part Two: That there is a Redeemer, demonstrated by Scripture.

(40)

The first chapter on humankind was to have been devoted to "Vanity," a major biblical theme: *Vanitas vanitatum, et omnia vanitas,* "Vanity of vanities, all is vanity," according to the first words of Ecclesiastes, denouncing the emptiness, the nothingness of the world and of men.

And the choice of a trade is, for Pascal, one of the best examples of human vanity: "Trade. / So many natures exist in man! So many vocations, and through so much chance! Everyone ordinarily takes up what he has heard praised. A well-crafted heel" (162).

We make up our minds on the basis of appearances. But let us not believe that the trade of mathematician or physicist, poet, or theologian escapes the law of vanity. Pascal knows that the quest for glory was not absent from his own scientific work, nor even from his pamphlet against the Jesuits, his *Provincial Letters,* the "little letters" to whose worldly success he was not insensitive. And we are caught up in the contradictions: If we do not act for glory, then we give in to inaction and indolence: "Glory. / Admiration spoils everything from childhood on. 'Oh, how well said! Oh, how well done! How well-behaved!' and so forth. The children of Port-Royal, who are not motivated by envy and glory, fall into indifference" (97).[1]

---

1. Port-Royal was a medieval abbey located south of Paris. It became known as Port-Royal-des-Champs after 1625, when most of the nuns moved to a new facility in Paris. It was the epicenter of Jansenism, a theological movement named after Dutch bishop Cornelius Jansen (1585–1638) that was deemed

By protecting oneself from one flaw (pride, the quest for glory), one falls into its opposite (idleness, indolence). Pascal observes this among the children of the Petites-Écoles of Port-Royal, trained in humility and lacking in aspiration. The middle ground is inaccessible to humans on their own.

---

heretical for its assertation that humans need not exercise free will to receive grace. The Port-Royal community included many remarkable intellectuals, including Pascal, who defended Jansenism in the Provincial Letters.

3

Amor Sui

       Self-love was the major theme for the moralists of the classical era—because that passion was reputed to be consuming, all-powerful, for fallen humankind. In the wake of the original sin, ever since Adam's transgression, the absence of God has created in the human heart an infinite void, impossible to fill with finite objects. Self-love has taken the place of love of God and of love for one's neighbor through God—that is, charity: "Just as I have loved you, you also should love one another," Christ commands in John's Gospel (13:34).[1] But charity struggles with the task, and it is self-love that rules the world, creaturely love, not the love of one's neighbor.

The issue of self-love comes up everywhere in the *Pensées*. "The nature of love and of the human self is that it loves only itself and considers only itself" (743). In his selfishness, a man cannot be

---

1. All biblical citations are from the New Revised Standard Version: https://www.pdfdrive.com/the-bible-new-revised-standard-version-e40079856.html.

unaware, however, that the object he loves is full of faults and wretchedness. Everything sends him back to his own fallen nature: "He wants to be great, and sees himself small. He wants to be happy, and sees himself miserable. He wants to be perfect, and sees himself full of imperfections. He wants to be the object of men's love and esteem, and he sees that his failings deserve only their dislike and contempt" (743).

But instead of convincing him of his state, this spectacle inspires in him "the most unrighteous and most criminal passion imaginable," and "he conceives a mortal hatred against this truth that admonishes him and convinces him of his faults" (743).

Self-love, which Pascal also calls concupiscence, is the opposite of charity; it is the creaturely love that no longer depends on the love of God. Pascal follows Saint Augustine, for whom it is the will that loves, in the sense that it desires and is almost magnetically attracted by its object. If this attraction is toward God, it produces charity; if it is toward a human creature, it produces lust. Love mobilizes the soul, gives it strength and life; it leads the soul toward its "natural place." "My weight is my love," *pondus meum amor meus,* Augustine says in his *Confessions* (13:9, p. 55). If Augustine speaks of "two loves," in truth only one exists for him, for charity and lust differ only through the object (God or creature).

After his father's death, in 1651, Pascal wrote a magnificent letter of consolation to his sister Gilberte and his brother-in-law Florin Périer. There is no better definition of self-love in his work:

> To conquer that horror more powerfully, it is essential to understand its origin; and to impress it on you in a few words, I am

obliged to tell you in general what is the source of all vices and all sins. . . . The truth that opens up this mystery is that God created man with two loves, one for God, the other for himself. . . . Man in that state not only loved himself without sin, but could not fail to love himself without sin. Since then, sin having arrived, man has lost the first of those loves; and the love of himself having remained . . . , that self-love has spread and overflowed in the void that the love of God has left behind. . . . This is the origin of self-love. It was natural to Adam, and just, in his innocence; but then it became both criminal and immoderate, in the aftermath of his sin. (*Œuvres complètes* 2:857–958; hereafter *OC*)

Before that sin, man knew the two loves innocently, but after the sin, man has been possessed by concupiscence, cut off from the love of God, given over entirely to the love of creatures, to *amor sui* (*OC* 3:793).

Pascal means first to humiliate humans, to curtail their self-love and then show them how to free themselves from it: he does this first by showing that religion is "worthy of veneration because it has understood man well"—that is, it has seen the wretchedness that man's self-love hides from him—then by showing that religion is "lovable because it promises the true good" (46). Which comes down, nevertheless, to flattering his self-love somewhat: "Let man judge his worth now. Let him love himself, for there is in him a nature capable of good; but let him not, on that account, love what is base in himself. Let him despise himself, because this capacity is empty; but let him not, on that account, despise this natural capacity. Let him hate himself; let him love himself. He has within himself the capability of knowing truth and being happy" (151).

And there we have a first example of the coincidence of opposites, an essential component of Pascal's thought.

4

"Mistress of Error and Falsehood"

The "Apology for the Christian Religion" that the *Pensées* sketches out was to offer a therapy for atheists. Pascal wanted to cure them of their ills, treat their malady of self-love, illusion, and self-deceiving blindness. His aim was to confront evil with its own tactics by shaking up his patients, humiliating and bullying them, by showing them their true nature: "If he exalts himself, I humble him. / If he humbles himself, I exalt him. / And I continue to contradict him / Until he comprehends / That he is an incomprehensible monster" (163). Or again: "Know then, proud man, what a paradox you are to yourself. Humble yourself, powerless reason. Be silent, dumb nature" (164).

The intent was to destroy the narcissism of his interlocutors, to eradicate their trust in themselves.

Now, the best auxiliary of the vanity that hides humans' wretchedness from themselves is their imagination, a faculty that Pascal doesn't hesitate to describe as "mistress of error and falsehood": "The imagination has a particular feature: it produces the greatest things with as little effort and time as the small ones," he wrote as early as 1647 to Father Noël, a scholar with whom he engaged in a polemic about the horror of the void (*OC* 2:522).

To illustrate the wretchedness, vanity, weakness, and impotence of humans without God, a lengthy fragment from the sheaf "Vanity" situates the imagination, fueled by opinions, as the lowest of faculties in the Platonic tradition: "That arrogant power, the enemy of reason, which it enjoys controlling and dominating so as to show how all-powerful it is, has established a second nature in man. It has its happy ones, its unhappy, its healthy, its sick, its rich and its poor. It makes them believe, doubt, and deny reason. It suppresses the senses; it arouses them. It has its fools and its wise men, and nothing vexes us more than to see it fill its hosts with a fuller and more complete satisfaction than reason" (78).

Imagination creates disproportions, enlarging what is small and vice versa: "The imagination enlarges small objects to the point of filling our souls with a fantastic exaggeration, and with bold insolence it reduces great objects down to its own level, as when speaking of God" (461).

Pascal began his battle against imagination as a man of science, by proving the existence of the vacuum and by refuting the fantasies of the physicists who had believed, since Aristotle's day, that "nature abhors a vacuum." In fact, "Nature has no distaste for a void," Pascal wrote in 1648 in the preface to his "Account of the Great Experiment on the Equilibrium of Liquids": "She [nature] makes no effort to avoid it; . . . all the effects that have been attributed to that horror stem from the weight and pressure of the air. . . . This is the sole and true cause, and . . . since this was not known, that imaginary abhorrence of the void had been deliberately invented to account for it" (*OC* 2:688).

For Pascal, the vacuum was a fact, observable in a glass tube above a column of mercury balanced by the weight of the air, by atmospheric pressure. And he did not hesitate to counter Descartes head on: "When men's weakness has been unable to find the real causes, their subtlety has substituted imaginary ones, which they have expressed by specious names that fill the ears but not the mind: thus they say that the sympathy and antipathy of natural bodies are the efficient and univocal causes of several effects, as if inanimate bodies were capable of sympathy and antipathy" (*OC* 2:688).

Later, making himself an apologist for religion, Pascal would by no means abandon the sciences. But his struggle against the vanity of man, who is deceived by his imagination instead of reasoning, began during his research on vacuums. Still, as always with Pascal, there is an "opposite truth" (479), and imagination, as we shall see, plays a providential role in the institution of political order.

5

"The Life of Monsieur Pascal"

Shortly after Pascal's death, Gilberte Périer, his older sister, drafted "The Life of Monsieur Pascal" to serve as the preface to an edition of the *Pensées*. This biography, left out of the first editions published by Port-Royal in 1670 and 1678, appeared in the 1658 edition. It is the hagiography of an exceptionally gifted individual: "As soon as my brother was old enough for us to talk to him, he gave evidence of a highly extraordinary mind through the brief, completely appropriate responses he gave, but even more so through the questions he asked about the nature of things, which surprised everyone" (*OC* 1:571).

Blaise Pascal, like his sisters Gilberte (three years older) and Jacqueline (two years younger), never went to school. After their mother died in 1626, when Blaise was three years old, their father, a legal scholar and a mathematician, resigned from his positions and took charge of their education. He left Clermont in 1631 and moved to Paris, where he frequented the best scholars and introduced his young son to them.

The family legend has it that Pascal reinvented Euclidean geometry on his own, up to the thirty-second proposition (the sum of the angles of any triangle is equal to two right angles), at an age when his father was introducing him exclusively to ancient languages. It seems more probable that the child had secretly read a treatise in geometry belonging to his father, who then discovered and marveled at his son's genius.

The prodigy forged ahead along this fine path, and "at age sixteen," Gilberte says, "he produced a treatise on conic sections that was taken to be such a major effort of the mind that people said nothing so powerful had been seen since Archimedes" (*OC* 1:576). This was his first publication, in 1640. "During all that time, he kept on learning Latin and he also learned Greek; and beyond that, during and after meals, my father spoke to him sometimes about logic, sometimes about physics and the other parts of philosophy; and this is all he learned about these subjects, having never been to school or had any other master for that any more than for the rest" (*OC* 1:576).

Later, the learned doctors at the Sorbonne reproached him for being an autodidact: "M. Pascal knew about Scripture only what the others taught him. . . . He hardly knew any Latin. He was not a scholar; he was a worldly dilettante" (*OC* 1:894). The accusation was unjust, for Pascal had a very good understanding of theology.

Gilberte referred to her brother's poor health and the daily pains that bothered him for most of his life. What is fascinating in this short career is the speed with which Pascal passed from one object of curiosity to another, leaving each one as soon as he had solved the challenge it posed for contemporary scholars.

Again, according to the legend, he passed through three periods in his life at an accelerated rhythm: first, a scientific period, in his youth, from 1640 to 1651; second, a secular period, from 1648 to 1654; last, a pious period, from age thirty on, starting with the "night of fire" of November 1654 and continuing up to his death at age thirty-nine.

But the periods overlap. Pascal continued to improve his arithmetic machine, the ancestor of the calculator, between 1642 and 1649, a time when, as gifted for worldly pursuits as for the sciences, he had acquired, according to Gilberte, "the air and the manners of the [social] world with as much assurance as if he had been nourished by them all his life" (*OC* 1:612). While he distanced himself from his sister Jacqueline, who joined Port-Royal right after the death of their father in 1651, he became close to her again starting in 1653. And it was in the middle of his religious period, after the *Provincial Letters,* in 1658, that he issued a challenge to European scientists concerning the problems posed by the cycloid.

Hence, Gilberte was exaggerating when she noted that Pascal renounced science at age twenty-three after his experiments with vacuums: "That occupation was the last in which he applied his mind to the human sciences" (*OC* 1:577). No, Pascal went on to invent, or to prefigure, the calculation of probabilities, which he called the "geometry of chance" in his treatise on the arithmetic triangle in 1654.

If he began to feel "an extreme aversion to the follies and the amusements of the world" in late 1653, as Jacqueline confided to Gilberte in a letter written in January 1655 (*OC* 3:71), his piety did not prevent him from pursuing activities as a businessman with his friend the duc de Roannez, such as drying out swamps in the Poitevin region or, in 1662, starting an inexpensive carriage service, the first public transportation business in Paris and a very profitable investment.

According to Gilberte again, "not only did he have no attachment to others, but he had no desire at all for others to be attached to him" (*OC* 1:592). Still, Pascal, the exceptionally gifted child, the eternal adolescent (*puer senex*), never left the core of the family, and his sister Jacqueline was probably his greatest love.

6

"The Queen of the World"

Here is another enigmatic fragment of the *Pensées:* "He has four lackeys" (53). Pascal made a note for himself so he would remember. Having four lackeys is an example of "Vanity," an illustration of the glory, or vainglory, that a man finds in showing himself to be a man of stature, impressing people with his domestic retinue.

But the same example comes up again a bit further on, in the sheaf labeled "Cause of Effects." This is one of the subtlest notions Pascal develops in the *Pensées.* A practice that initially strikes us as arbitrary, vain, unreasonable—for example, a man walking down the streets of Paris with four lackeys to show off the extent of his household—becomes, if one gives it more thought, an effect that is not without reason, that has its cause, a reason and a cause that confer legitimacy on it. Pascal, a nuanced dialectician, is always seeking to cross through the mirror in order to discover "the causes for effects": "This is remarkable. They do not want me to honor a man dressed in brocade and followed by seven or eight lackeys. And yet, he will have me thrashed, if I do not salute him. His garb is power" (53).

Pascal observes first of all the disproportion, or the hiatus, the non sequitur there is between the cause and the effect: The man is surrounded by lackeys, therefore I salute him, I bow, and I do this apparently without reason. But no, in reality the lackeys are not insignificant; they mean something and not nothing, and they display a might that imposes respect: if I fail to salute the man, I will get a whipping.

Thus, Pascal uses a striking example to introduce a whole series of reflections, still provocative today, on the relationship between justice and might. For justice yields to might. Ideally, the just ought to be the strong ones, but in reality the strong are the ones who impose themselves as just, by way of four, seven, or eight lackeys. The substitution of the mighty for the just, the usurpation of justice by force is initially presented as a sign of the "wretchedness" of the world and the "vanity" of human beings. But, thanks to the discovery of the "reason for effects," introducing a dialectical nuance that Pascal will also call "gradation" or "thought in the back of the mind," what appeared first to be an aberration turns out upon closer examination to be a necessity, justified at a higher, or deeper, level by a sort of passage to the second degree. Since the just don't know how to be strong, the strong really have to be just, or have to pass for just, in order for society to be maintained. What gives legitimacy to the power of force over justice is that force stabilizes the political and social order:

> It is just that the just be followed. It is necessary that the strongest be followed. / Justice without might is impotent. / Might

without justice is tyrannical. Justice without might is contested, because there are always evil people. / Might without justice is indicted. Thus justice and might must be brought together, and to do that is to make the just strong, or to make the strong just. / Justice is subject to dispute. Might is eminently recognizable and indisputable. And so, we have been unable to ensure that what is strong is just, because might has challenged justice, calling it unjust while calling itself just. / And thus, being unable to ensure that what is just is mighty, we have made what is mighty just (135).

All of Pascal's political thought is summed up here: nothing justifies the established order, but nothing justifies changing it since that would risk provoking a civil war; power is legitimate not because it is just but because it is established. "Being unable to strengthen justice, we have justified might, so that justice and might could coexist and there could be peace, which is the supreme good" (116).

Such a philosophy may strike us as conservative and cynical, but Pascal, along with his father and his sisters, feared for their lives during the Fronde;[1] it disrupted public order but was ultimately unsuccessful. From May 1649 to November 1650, Étienne Pascal, Blaise, and Jacqueline left Paris in turn and took refuge in Clermont. In the *Pensées,* Pascal explicitly denounced "the injustice of the Fronde, which raises its alleged justice against might" (119). However, he never showed hostility to royal authority or to absolute monarchy. "The art of revolution is to disrupt established customs," as he put it, "a game that is sure to ruin everything" (94).

1. The Fronde was a popular uprising in the mid-seventeenth century that opposed the growing power of the monarchy.

7

"On the Art of Persuasion"

"Real eloquence cares little for eloquence" (671). This fragment of the *Pensées* is often cited without any reference to the author. The idea was fashionable in Pascal's day. An honnête homme should conduct himself in a casual manner, with the *negligentia diligens,* or "diligent negligence," that had been cultivated by men at court since the Renaissance. While rhetorical flourishes come across as academic and artificial, the art of true eloquence conceals itself. Pascal, under the cover of naturalness, knew all the means of persuasion.

Another fragment of the *Pensées* spells out his doctrine: "Eloquence / It requires something that is agreeable and real, but the agreeable itself has to be grounded in truth" (547).

Pascal did not reject agreeableness. He saw the ability to please as indispensable. This accounts for the extraordinary success of his *Provincial Letters,* in which he proved capable of debating arduous questions concerning dogmatics and casuistry in the tone found in salons while being funny too.

He had reflected on the conditions of an eloquence that is both pleasing and truthful well before plunging into polemics. He had already set down on paper some considerations on the geometric mind and on the art of persuasion. So he had a method he could use in both literary and scientific contexts: "No one is unaware that there are two entrances through which opinions are received in the soul, understanding and will, which are the soul's two principal powers. The most natural is that of understanding, for one should never consent to anything but demonstrated truths; but the most ordinary, although against nature, is that of will; for all the men in the world are almost always led to believe not by proof but by agreeableness" (*OC* 3:413).

Pascal knew well that in the domain of discourse, unlike that of the sciences, proof, which is addressed to understanding, is not enough; enjoyment is also needed, and this involves will. He understands "will," the second entry point to the soul, in a very broad sense, the way Saint Augustine understood *voluntas:* it is the *impetus actionis,* the impulse toward action. It thus includes desire; today, we would say that it includes involuntary as well as voluntary impulses. And Pascal recognizes that enjoyment does not have the same value as proof—that will is thus an inferior choice: "This path is lowly, unworthy, and foreign; thus everyone disavows it. . . . I am speaking then only of the truths within our reach; and it is of these that I say that the mind and the heart are like doors through which they are received into the soul, but that few enter by way of the mind, rather they are introduced in large numbers by the bold whims of the will, without the counsel of reasoning" (*OC* 3:413–414).

The new distinction between the mind and the heart follows from the distinction between the understanding and the will. And the will, like the heart, is capricious. It is mobilized by certain natural desires common to all men, such as the desire to be happy. According to Pascal, "All men want to be happy. There are no exceptions, no matter what means they use. They all strive toward this goal" (181). So much so that for all of us there are objects that, "having the power to please us, are strong enough, although pernicious in effect, to prod the will into action, as if they were producing real happiness" (OC 3:415).

This is why Pascal means to act on both understanding and will, with one's mind and one's heart, since there is no way to get around will: "It seems that here, whatever the point about which one wants to convince someone else, one must be attentive to that person: one must know his mind and heart, what principles he accepts, what things he loves; and then one must notice, for the matter in question, what relations it has with the acknowledged principles or with the objects made attractive by the charms one attributes to them. So that the art of persuasion consists as much in pleasing as in convincing, given the extent to which men are governed more by caprice than by reason!" (OC 3:416).

Pascal will thus adapt reason to enjoyment; he will combine the art of convincing, which is addressed to the mind, with the art of pleasing, which targets will, desire, or pleasure.

But his "De l'art de persuader" ("On the Art of Persuasion") concerns only natural truths, not first principles or supernatural truths, which are accessible solely via the heart: "I am not speaking here of divine truths, which I would take care not to ascribe to the art of persuasion, for they are infinitely above nature. God alone can place them in the soul, and in whatever manner he pleases" (*OC* 3:413).

Later, in the *Pensées,* the distinction will be between the heart and reason: "We know truth not only through reason but also through the heart; it is via the latter that we know first principles, and reason, which plays no role here, tries in vain to challenge those principles" (142).

The point of view has changed. Reason governs the linking of propositions, but it has no access to the primary principles. The principles of knowledge come from the heart, as do the ultimate ends.

8

Tyranny

Tyranny is a major Pascalian theme. If Pascal, thanks to a "thought in the back of the mind," respects might and, since it guarantees order, judges it legitimate even when it is imposed at the expense of justice, he still stands up against tyranny, which he defines in the *Pensées:* "Tyranny consists in the universal desire for domination beyond one's own order" (92).

Tyranny is an illegitimate force because it exercises its authority in a domain that does not fall under its competence or jurisdiction. It is thus an abuse of power. So political authority cannot legitimately impose itself in scientific, artistic, intellectual, or religious matters, for these matters belong to different orders: "There are various niches occupied by the strong, the handsome, the judicious, the pious; each of them rules in his own place but not elsewhere, and sometimes they meet. And the strong and the handsome fight foolishly to see who will be master; but their mastery is of different sorts. They do not understand one another, and their failing is that each seeks to rule everywhere. Nothing allows this, not even might, for might is of no use in the realm of learning; it governs only external actions" (92).

There is no reason for any contest between might and beauty, or might and science, or might and religion. A tyrannical order is one that purports to "reign everywhere," including outside of its own domain.

For Pascal, the tyranny at issue was first of all that of the pope, who wanted Port-Royal to recognize publicly that Jansen's doctrine could be found in the five propositions condemned on May 31, 1653, by the papal bull *Cum occasione* (here we enter into the lengthy, complicated quarrel in which the Jansenists opposed papal authority). As Pascal wrote in the seventeenth and next-to-last *Provincial Letter:* "How could doctors, who are convinced that Jansen meant nothing but efficacious grace, possibly consent to a declaration that they condemn his doctrine without an explanation of it, since given what they believe about it, from which no one has converted them, this would simply amount to condemning efficacious grace, which cannot be condemned without sinning. Would it not therefore be strangely tyrannical to put them into the unhappy position of having either to become guilty before God, if they signed such a declaration against their conscience, or to be treated as heretics if they refused to do so?"[1]

In 1649, the Sorbonne attacked the Jansenist theses derived from the Augustinus, Jansen's work on grace. In brief, the Jan-

1. *Pascal: The Provincial Letters,* translated by A. J. Krailsheimer, p. 275.
Subsequent references will be identified by the abbreviation *PL* followed by the letter number and page number.

senists argued that a Christian could not be saved without the intervention of efficacious grace, whereas the Jesuits maintained that sufficient grace, as the name indicates, was enough. Port-Royal agreed to condemn the propositions as heretical while denying that they could be found in Jansen. Rome settled the question with the bull that attributed all five to Jansen. The distinction between law and fact, behind which Port-Royal was taking refuge, fell away.

Pascal is still thinking about abuses of papal authority when he describes tyranny in the "Wretchedness" sheaf of the *Pensées:* "Tyranny means seeking to take by one path something that one can only have by another. . . . Thus statements like the following are false and tyrannical: 'I am handsome, so I ought to be feared. I am strong, so I ought to be loved. I am . . .' etc. And it is similarly false and tyrannical to say: 'He is not strong, so I shall not respect him. He is not clever, so I shall not fear him'" (91).

We are back to the tyranny of the Fronde, which also unsettled the orders of society.

If Pascal sees tyranny at work in the pope's exertion of authority on doctrinal matters, however, he does not impute tyranny to absolute monarchy, which preserves order. Tyranny is an attack on what is not yet called freedom of expression or freedom of thought, and Pascal's fight against tyranny prefigures the modern notion of tolerance. This explains why, in the eyes of certain Catholics, including those associated with Port-Royal, Pascal, even if he sought to convert libertines, was doing impious work, for he committed himself, for better or for worse, to the side of those who encouraged freedom of conscience against religion.

9

Casuistry

Pascal led a long, hard fight against the casuists in the *Provincial Letters,* but also in the *Pensées,* where we read that "the Christian religion in the Holy Books is very different from the casuists' version" (276). In other words, the casuists were perverting the religion of the Gospel.

But who were the casuists? They were theologians, Jesuits in particular, who analyzed and resolved problems of conscience, moral problems. In the *Provincial Letters,* Pascal inveighed against their laxity, for they permitted almost everything under certain conditions. They cleverly twisted the prohibitions pronounced by the Church.

According to this note in the *Pensées* intended for the *Provincial Letters:* "The casuists submit decisions to reason, which is corrupt, and the choice of decisions to will, also corrupt, so that everything that is corrupt in human nature plays a role in human conduct" (498).

In the *Provincial Letters,* Pascal brings the mockers around to his side, by showing that the casuists allow all crimes. For example, the king's edicts forbade dueling, and of course God's commandments did the same, but there will always be a casuist—Molina, the most famous Spanish Jesuit theologian, or another, Hurtado, Escobar, Sanchez, or Lessius—who permits dueling if one does not have "the express intention of fighting": "For what harm can there be in going to a field, walking about waiting for someone and defending one-self if attacked?" (*PL* 7, p. 106).

Thus, dueling, if it arises as an accidental, rather than premeditated, meeting, is allowed thanks to a mental restriction that in Pascal's eyes is only a subterfuge, an act of wordplay.

The argument against the casuists is brilliant. Pascal freely multiplies quotations from the casuists defending opinions that good sense deems absurd—for example, statements that defend homicide under certain circumstances but also usury, for "it would be usury to make a profit from those to whom one lends if one demands it as legally due, but if one demands it as due out of gratitude, it is not usury" (*PL* 8, p. 121). The same for simony, buying or selling a clerical position or something of a spiritual nature, "if the money is given as a motive inducing the incumbent to resign the benefice" (*PL* 6, p. 94), and for vengeance, for "someone who has been slapped may not have the intention of avenging himself; but he may very well have that of avoiding infamy, and to that end repel such an insult at once, even at the point of the sword" (*PL* 7, pp. 90–91). Casuists have even justified sodomy (*PL* 6) or priests who maliciously say mass while in a state of mortal sin (604).

To the casuists who claim that "someone who has been slapped may pursue his enemy forthwith, not to avenge himself but to redeem his honour" (*PL* 13, p. 193) or that "one may kill for a slap"

(*PL* 13, p. 206), Pascal, who addresses these cases at length, objects: "According to St. Augustine, . . . 'whoever kills a criminal without authority becomes criminal himself, chiefly because he is usurping authority which God has not given him'; and on the contrary, judges who do have such authority are still murderers if they cause the death of an innocent man against the laws which they should observe" (*PL* 14, p. 209). Here we find Pascal respectful of established authorities and legitimate force, long before Max Weber's thesis on the processes of civilizing societies through the institution of state monopoly over legitimate violence. "Who then empowered you to say, as do Molina, Reginaldus, Filiutius, Escobar, Lessius and the others: 'It is permissible to kill someone who comes to strike us'? . . . By what authority do you, who are only private individuals, bestow this power of killing on individuals and even religious [officials]?" (*PL* 14, p. 211).

Let us not jump to the conclusion that Pascal denies all validity to casuistry. What he challenges is the laxity that, in the name of probabilism, authorizes one to accept a probable opinion that has been issued by a theologian on dueling, vengeance, simony, or sodomy, even though other opinions may be more probable—for example, that of Saint Augustine. "Probability. [The casuists] have some real principles, but they abuse them" (451).

10

The Father

We know very little about Pascal's mother, who died when he was three years old. But his father was an impressive figure, omnipresent, all-powerful. Pascal respected authority, starting with his father's, but it was surely not easy to be the son of such a father.

Étienne Pascal (1588–1651) was a legal scholar, a mathematician, and a musician. As a law student in Paris, he is thought to have frequented the lawyer Antoine Arnauld (1560–1619), the father of a whole Port-Royal clan: Robert Arnauld d'Andilly (1589–1674), state counsellor and a solitary of Port-Royal;[1] Catherine Arnauld (1590–1651); Mother Angélique (1591–1661), the Port-Royal reformer; Mother Agnès (1593–1671), who succeeded Mother Angélique as the Port-Royal abbess; Henri Arnauld, bishop of Angers (1597–1692); and, finally, Antoine Arnauld (1612–1694), the Grand Arnauld,

---

1. The solitaries were men who chose to live as hermits at Port-Royal-des-Champs.

the doctrinarian of Jansenism. And we must not forget that Antoine Le Maistre, the first solitary of Port-Royal, and Louis-Isaac Lemaistre de Sacy, translator of the Bible, were sons of Catherine Arnauld.

The Pascal family, which converted to Jansenism in 1646, belonged to the same milieu as the Arnaulds, the hereditary *noblesse de robe* in the Auvergne region, partisans of an austere Catholicism and a rigoristic morality.

When his son was born in 1623, Étienne Pascal was a counsellor at the Court of Aids[2] in Clermont; later, he became second president of the Court of Aids of Montferrand. At age forty-three, in 1631, he retired to Paris in order to frequent the best scholars and educate his children. Having protested against the lowering of his income by the City of Paris in 1638, he had to shift into a clandestine existence before being rescued by his daughter Jacqueline, whose poetic talent allowed the family to get back into Richelieu's good graces. He joined the cardinal's staff and in 1640 became the king's commissioner for the imposition of taxes in Rouen, a wealthy, conquered province; he excelled in that activity, and it incited his son to invent his arithmetic machine. Étienne Pascal was thus first an officer, holder of a charge that he sold, then an intendant, an agent of royal power in a province, named in a royal commission.

He had "great affection" for his "only son," Périer was to say ("La vie de Monsieur Pascal," p. 571; hereafter "La vie"), but he was an authoritarian and possessive man, an incorruptible magistrate yet hard

---

2. The Cour des Aides was a public court that dealt with customs and fiscal matters.

and intransigent; a learned and powerful man gifted in accounting and finance but fair and honest, he was his children's only teacher.

All three, whom he controlled until his death, were exceptional. In 1641 Gilberte, his oldest daughter, married Florin Périer, a cousin of Étienne's whom the latter had brought to Rouen to be the second in command in his commission; Périer left with his wife for Clermont-Ferrand in 1642.

In 1646, in Rouen, a fall immobilized Étienne and put the family in contact with the faithful at Port-Royal, who brought into their fold first the son, then the father, then the youngest daughter. Their conversion to Jansenism did not lead them to renounce the secular world or to join the opposition. Étienne Pascal remained an intendant until 1648, at the point in the Fronde when the position of commissioner was abolished. With no sympathy for the Fronde, the family aligned with the royal court and, like Pascal's friend the duc de Roannez, they defended the legitimacy of the monarchy.

Jacqueline, an excellent poet, soon expressed the wish to withdraw to Port-Royal, where one could be a nun "reasonably," she said, according to her sister Gilberte ("Vie de Jacqueline Pascal," p. 664). Étienne Pascal felt betrayed by his children: "He even complained about my brother," Gilberte said, "for having fomented this plan without knowing whether it would be agreeable to him [Étienne]; and that consideration embittered him so against my brother and sister that he no longer trusted them" ("La vie," p. 665). He gave up the idea of finding Jacqueline a husband, but he refused to allow her to follow her vocation before he died. In 1651, Pascal in turn resisted his sister's departure for Port-Royal.

On that occasion, Gilberte and Jacqueline conspired behind his back ("Vie de Jacqueline Pascal," p. 671).

The Pascal clan was exceptional, with an affectionate but imperious father; an "impatient" son, according to Gilberte, reporting the words of the curate of Saint-Étienne-du-Mont who accompanied him in his final illness ("He's a child," the priest said ["La vie," p. 596]); a willful younger daughter; and an older daughter who survived them all and providentially transmitted their memory with an impeccable command of the language.

If Blaise Pascal was an eternal child, the letter of consolation he sent to his sister Gilberte and his brother-in-law on the death of his father attested to his great Augustinian theological maturity at a point that is nevertheless most often associated with his secular period.

11

"I Find It Fitting That Copernicus's Opinion Not Be Closely Analyzed"

Pascal grew up among scholars. From early childhood on, he accompanied his father to sessions at Father Mersenne's academy. In this scientific salon, he met the mathematician Gilles de Roberval, the philosopher René Descartes, the philosopher and scientist Pierre Gassendi. And he corresponded at an early age with the mathematician Pierre de Fermat.

It was a critical period for the history of science. Scientific experiments were questioning Aristotelian scholastics—for example, the abhorrence of vacuums. Weight had been an object of great curiosity for many before Newton's laws offered an explanation. Copernicus had put the sun at the center of the universe and hypothesized that the planets turn around it and also rotate themselves. Kepler had shown that planetary orbits were ellipses rather than circles. Galileo had formulated the first mathematical law of the new physics: the speed with which an object falls is independent of its mass.

Pascal lived at the precise moment when the vision of the world was being overturned: he witnessed the scientific revolution that broke with the image of the world inherited from the Bible and Aristotle and brought about the shift from "the closed world to the infinite universe," in Alexandre Koyré's words—from the closed world of the ancient philosophers and the Middle Ages to the infinite universe of the moderns.

A quite understandable panic ensued, a reaction that Pascal dramatized in the *Pensées* in order to frighten the libertines. But from the outset he was sensitive to the lack of comprehension that had arisen between science and faith, in the wake of the theories advanced by Copernicus, Kepler, and Galileo. One feature of papal tyranny, as Pascal saw it, was the condemnation of Galileo in 1633, to which the Jesuits were thought to have contributed. This became a motif of the polemic in the *Provincial Letters* against their order:

> It was in vain too that you obtained from Rome the decree against Galileo, which condemned his opinion regarding the earth's movement. It will take more than that to prove that it keeps still, and if there were consistent observations proving that it is the earth that goes round, all the men in the world put together could not stop it turning, or themselves turning with it. (*PL* 18, pp. 295–296)

The passage recalls the no doubt apocryphal formula attributed to Galileo after he recanted: *Eppur si muove!* (And yet it moves!). But Pascal is prudent: he presents Galileo's theory as an "opinion," thus as a hypothesis rather than a certainty. He does not say that the earth turns around the sun. Instead, he resorts to a wise conditional: if experience were to prove that the earth turns, the condemnations of the Inquisition would not prevent it from turning. There was nevertheless hardly any doubt about the question in the Parisian scientific circles that Pascal frequented in the 1650s.

His reserved approach can be explained not only by his scientific rigor but also by his intention to remind scientists of the vanity of their science. This is how one can understand the following fragment in the *Pensées:* "I find it fitting that Copernicus's opinion not be closely analyzed" (196).

Scientific research is a diversion of the same sort as hunting or gambling, for it distracts from what is essential, the search for supernatural truth. In the preceding fragment of the *Pensées,* Pascal compares the libertine to a prisoner in a cell who has one hour left to determine whether his death warrant has been signed and try to get it revoked but spends that hour playing cards (195).

In the long fragment of the *Pensées* on "Diversions" in which Pascal lists the "diverse agitations" that allow men to avoid thinking about their condition, he mentions those who "sweat in their offices to show the scholars that they have solved an algebra problem that couldn't have been solved before" (168). This is just what Pascal himself did again later, several years after his conversion, during his research on cycloids.

The pursuit of mathematics is a diversion like any other, such as poetry, for which his sister Jacqueline had a great "talent" that Port-Royal asked her to "bury" because it could have brought her "glory" (Périer, "Vie de Jacqueline Pascal," p. 668).

If Pascal does not choose between the Ptolemaic system and that of Copernicus, it is less due to timidity (for want of proofs) than to humility, for the universe is unquestionably infinite in his eyes, and even doubly infinite, as illustrated by the famous fragment on the "disproportion of man" (230).[1] In the face of that double infinitude, the controversy over the center of the world—the earth or the sun— loses all pertinence. If the world is infinite, the circumference is nowhere and the center is everywhere:

> The entire visible world is but an imperceptible feature in the ample bosom of nature; no idea comes close. It is no use inflating our conceptions beyond the imaginable spaces, we give birth only to atoms, at the price of the reality of things. It is an infinite sphere whose center is everywhere, its circumference nowhere. (230)

1. This long fragment contrasts human incomprehension of a universe at once infinitely great and infinitely small to an omniscient creator's divine intelligence.

12

Pascal and the Marxists

Marxists have always respected Pascal. They like his political cynicism, his offensive style, his dialectical virtuosity, his moral austerity, his purified faith. They make militants read the *Provincial Letters* to train them to fight their class enemies.

In the film *Ma nuit chez Maud,* the childhood friend whom the Catholic Jean-Louis Trintignant rediscovered in Clermont-Ferrand is a Marxist philosophy professor, played by Antoine Vitez. In a café, he launches into a long discussion about Pascal's wager. Vitez defends Pascal's argument by substituting a bet on the meaning of history for the wager about the existence of God. If one has to choose between these two hypotheses—history has no meaning or history has a meaning—and even if there is a 90 percent chance that history has no meaning and just a 10 percent chance that it is meaningful, it is still reasonable to bet on a better world. Every political commitment to change the world is based on a wager similar to Pascal's, whereas Pascal, like his father, demonstrated great political caution.

The most thorough Marxist reading of Pascal remains that of Lucien Goldmann, in *The Hidden God,* on Jansenism, Pascal, and Racine. Goldmann defines Jansenism by what he calls a "refusal of the world within the world" (p. 70), and he identifies it with the social class known as the *robins,* the lower strata of the *noblesse de robe* that had lost ground in class terms owing to the increased power of the absolute monarchy and state centralism. Officers who bore patrimonial titles found themselves in competition with the intendant commissioners, agents of royal power. The monarchy had been reinforced to the detriment of the parliaments and the officers, provoking irritation and hostility among the *robins,* the class to which the Pascal and Arnauld families belonged.

These downgraded dignitaries are sometimes thought to have taken refuge in Jansenism, as did the solitaries of Port-Royal. While there was indeed a link between the parliamentary milieu and Port-Royal (it remained in place until the French Revolution, so much so that the eighteenth-century Jansenists were accused of having worked toward the fall of the old regime), and while Port-Royal in effect constituted a kernel of opposition to absolute monarchy, under the Old Regime the acquisition of an official position remained the path to social advancement. Moreover, intendants were often recruited among the officers. Étienne Pascal, an officer who sold his position at the Court of Aids in Clermont so that he could retire to Paris, thus became an intendant commissioner of the king in Rouen a few years later, and his conversion to Jansenism in no way kept him from continuing to fulfill his appointed role with zeal.

Nor did the Jansenism of the Pascal family incite them to withdraw from the world, and the abundance of notarized acts relating to their property in Clermont and Paris attests to the concern they had for their patrimony. Long after his father's death, Blaise himself maintained the idea of marrying and procuring his own official position, but the modesty of his patrimony and income delayed and eventually nullified that project. And he never pursued the intention to join the solitaries of Port-Royal.

Lucien Goldmann saw a break at the time of the *Provincial Letters* between the remnants of hope on the part of the Jansenists and the tragic rejection of the world in the *Pensées,* between the fight against the Jesuits and the apology for Christianity. Goldmann took Pascal's confinement within piety as a confirmation of his own political and social analysis of Jansenism. Now, most of the fragments in the *Pensées* were written between the summer of 1656 and the following summer, at the same time as the *Letters.* The pamphlet and the apology were contemporary and remain inseparable, and the refutation of the Jesuits' casuistry in the *Provincial Letters* foreshadowed the anthropology of the *Pensées.* The polemic introduced the reflection on skepticism that was the starting point for the *Pensées* according to the 1658 outline, for Jesuit casuistry is a form of skepticism. The connection is manifest in the following fragment:

> Each thing here is partly true and partly false. The essential truth is not at all like that: it is wholly pure and wholly true. Mixing dishonors and annihilates it. Nothing is purely true, and so nothing is true if it is understood with respect to pure truth. It will be said that it is true that homicide is bad. Yes, for we are very familiar with what is evil and false. But what will be called good? Chastity? I say no, for the world would end. Marriage? No, continence is

better. Abstaining from killing? No, for the disorder would be hor-
rible, and the wicked would kill the good. Killing? No, for that
would destroy nature. We have neither truth nor good except in
part, and mixed with evil and falsity. (450)

We might well think we are reading the *Apology for Raymond
Sebond,* in which Montaigne piles up contradictions. However, if the
skepticism encountered in the *Provincial Letters* is indeed the premise
of the *Pensées,* Pascal does not abandon the search for truth, nor does
he confine himself to tragic despair. The *Pensées* note the misery of
man without God and asserts the hidden God; these two essential
Pascalian theses, found in the polemic, bring about the unity of the
apology, binding together the anthropology and the theology of the
two texts.

We are far from the class struggle between officers and commissioners, but over a long period of time, the Marxists learned how
to fight political combat from the *Provincial Letters.* Was Pascal not
in fact the true teacher of Louis Althusser?[1]

---

1. Louis Althusser (1918–1990) was an influential French Marxist philosopher
and theorist of class structure.

13

"The Eternal Silence of Those Infinite Spaces Terrifies Me"

"The eternal silence of those infinite spaces terrifies me" (233). Here is one of the most emblematic fragments in the *Pensées*, a first-person statement that we moderns take to be the expression of an intimate existential anguish.

Victor Cousin, in his "Report to the Academy" in 1843 asking for a new edition of the *Pensées*, exclaimed: "That sinister line that we encounter, separated from all the rest, is it not like a lugubrious cry surging up all of a sudden from the depths of the soul, in the desert of a world without God!"

Pascal represents the nonbeliever placed before the infinite world that resulted from the scientific revolution of the sixteenth and seventeenth centuries. The silence of the cosmic spaces breaks with the idea of a universe ordered according to the musical harmony of the spheres, and it imposes a tragic solitude.

The moderns have personalized this anguish, on the strength in particular of the later witness of an abbot who, addressing a young woman subject to imaginary terrors, relates an anecdote about Pascal: "That great mind always believed he saw an abyss on his left side and had a chair placed there to reassure himself." Baudelaire took inspiration from the passage in a sonnet, "The Abyss" ("Le gouffre"). From there we have a whole vulgate depicting Pascal as nervous, neurotic, manic-depressive. The troubles of his early childhood were related by his niece, Marguerite Périer, who depicted him as in poor health throughout his life, afflicted with paralysis, aphonia, and migraines. These stories nourished the idea, widely accepted in the nineteenth century, that genius was linked to madness. They allowed Voltaire to conclude as early as 1741 that melancholy had led Pascal's reason astray and that his mental disorder accounted for his conversion.

Chateaubriand took the opposite view from Voltaire's in his *Genius of Christianity:* "It is difficult not to be overwhelmed with astonishment when, on opening the Thoughts of the Christian philosopher, we light upon the six chapters in which he treats of the nature of humankind. The sentiments of Pascal are particularly remarkable for their profound melancholy and a certain immensity which I cannot describe: you are suspended among these sentiments as in the midst of infinity" (p. 412).

From there we can follow the spread of a Romantic reading of man's wretchedness and vanity as a generalized soul-sickness, Romantic despair, and later the existential absurd; the *via veritas,* the path of truth, had been abandoned:

> It is like the ruins of Palmyra, the superb relics of genius and of past ages, at the foot of which the Arab of the desert has built his miserable hut. "Pascal," says Voltaire, "a sublime madman, born a century

too early." The significance of this *century too early* must be obvious
to every reader. . . . In what part of his works has the recluse of Port-
Royal soared above the greatest geniuses? In his six chapters on
man. Now these six chapters, which turn entirely on the original fall
of man, *would not exist had Pascal been an unbeliever.* (*Genius,* p. 412)

Chateaubriand, like Voltaire, chose to ignore the fact that Pascal
meant to arouse fright in his libertine interlocutor, shake him up,
shove him around, drag him out of his comfortable indifference, de-
liver him up to his anxiety.

Only Valéry, in his famous "Variation on a 'Pensée'" in 1923,
showed serious reservations: "I cannot help suspecting that there
is something systematic and labored about his attitude of perfect
misery, this absolute disgust. A well-turned sentence is incompat-
ible with total renunciation. A distress that writes so well is not so
complete that it hasn't salvaged some freedom of mind from the
shipwreck" (9:93). Valéry marks his distance in a singular way, un-
scathed by philosophy or religion: "I see Pascal's hand all too clearly"
(9:94). "One remembers in what terms . . . he allowed himself to
talk about Pascal," Nathalie Sarraute asserted reproachfully in 1947,
suspecting Valéry of feeling "the satisfaction of 'sinking his nail'
into Pascal" (*Paul Valéry et l'Enfant d'Éléphant,* pp. 56–57).

Still, the spectacle of the infinite universe can be distressing even
to a Christian:

When I consider the short duration of my life absorbed in the preceding and following eternity . . . the small space that I fill and
even that I see, crushed in the infinite immensity of the spaces

that I do not know and that do not know me, I am terrified and astonished to see myself here rather than there, for there is no reason why here rather than there, why now rather than then. Who put me here? By whose order and action have this place and this time been become my destiny? (102)

Nothing justifies my life, from my birth to my death:

I don't know who put me in the world, nor what the world is, nor what I am. I am in terrible ignorance of all things. . . . I see those terrifying spaces that enclose me in the universe, and I find myself attached to a corner of this vast expanse, without knowing why I am placed in this place rather than in another, nor why this small amount of time I am given to live is assigned to me at this point rather than another of all the eternity that has come before and all that follows. I see only infinities everywhere that enclose me like an atom and like a shadow that lasts only an instant and does not return. / All I know is that I must soon die, but what I know least of all is that very death that I shall be unable to avoid. (681)

How can we be sure that Pascal did not share the terror of the character who speaks here in the first person?

14

Gradation

       Pascal, always a subtle dialectician, is a champion of the "shift from for to against," which he also calls "the cause of the effects" or a "thought in the back of the mind"; these are among his principal contributions to the art of argumentation. In one of the best examples of his method in the *Pensées,* he compares and praises natural ignorance and learned ignorance, opposing them to knowledge, or to pseudo-knowledge, which lies in between.

> The world [that is, the people, the commons] judges things well, for it is in natural ignorance, the true situation of mankind. The sciences have two extremities that meet. The first is the pure natural ignorance in which all people find themselves at birth. The other extremity is the one reached by the great souls that, having run through everything that men can know, discover that they know nothing and find themselves in the same ignorance from which they began. But it is a learned ignorance, which acknowledges itself. (117)

This proposition recalls the connection Montaigne made between elementary-level ignorance, devoid of scientific knowledge, and doctoral-level ignorance, that of Socrates, which is attained after science. Montaigne added that the "half-breeds," located between the two, were "dangerous, inept, and importunate," for "these men trouble the world" (*Essays,* bk. 1, chap. 54, p. 276). Pascal adopts, for the moment, that hierarchy or "gradation," as he calls it:

> The ones in between, who have left natural ignorance behind but have not been able to reach the other, have a touch of that self-sufficient science and behave as if they understood. Those persons disturb the world and judge everything badly. Ordinary and clever people establish the ways of the world, the ones in between scorn the world and are scorned by it. They judge everything badly, and the world judges well. (117)

The people are better judges than those situated in between, who know a little about a subject, but not enough, and believe they know everything. As he often does, Pascal begins by defending a paradox: according to common opinion, the *doxa,* ignorance makes one either judge badly or be incapable of judging at all, while instruction allows one to make good judgments.

No, Pascal maintains the contrary thesis: the people can be right, even if they don't know why this is so (126). The idea is not new: it is the notion of the "erudite ignorance" of the humble, a theme that is both Socratic and Christian.

Pascal does not name those who are "in between." But the libertines are among the semiclever who believe that they are knowledgeable and scorn the people when they themselves are wrong. The people hold them in contempt in return, and Pascal shares their suspicion of the semiclever.

Here, like Montaigne, Pascal observes three degrees in the gradation of minds. Later he will distinguish five, adding the devout and the perfect Christians. With five degrees, the gradation becomes more elaborate and more original, properly Pascalian. On the topic of the respect owed to those who are by birth the greats of this world, Pascal identifies five forms of behavior characteristic of the ranks below, alternating between honor and scorn:

> Cause of the effects. / Gradation. The people honor persons of high birth. The semi-clever scorn them, saying that birth is not an advantage of the person, but a matter of chance. The clever honor them, not through the thinking of the people but through their own thoughts in the back of the mind. The devout, who have more zeal than science, scorn them, despite the consideration that makes the clever honor them, because they judge by a new light given them by their piety. But the perfect Christians honor them by another, higher light. / Thus the successive opinions go from for to against, depending on the light. (124)

The people believe naively that the laws are just and that those who are great by birth are superior; they judge essence according to appearance. The semiclever, disillusioned, distinguish being from appearing; they attribute social condition to chance and conclude that the great are to be scorned. The clever are not dupes of the gap between personal nature and social status. However, by a "more elevated" way of thinking, they grant external marks of respect to the great while privately withholding their esteem—but they are still respectful.

Up to this point, intelligence has presided over the ranking, but now faith takes over. Devout persons are semiclever in matters of faith. Taking Christian values literally, they confuse the city of men with the city of God, and they disapprove of the established social order. By contrast, perfect Christians are clever people who also have faith: they know that great men are sinners like everyone else, but they respect the will of God.

There is no better illustration of the "cause for effects" than these "thoughts in the back of the mind" that legitimize customs and show the "very healthy opinions" of the people, for example, for

> having chosen diversions, and hunting rather than killing. The semiclever make fun of them, and triumph in showing, on this point, the folly of the world. But for a reason that they themselves do not grasp, the people are right. (134)

So the world is not as foolish as it looks; Pascal finds its hidden order.

15

Violence and Truth

The contradictions between might and justice are a recurrent motif in Pascal's thought. He did not approve of the Fronde, which, as we have seen, "elevates its so-called justice against might" (119). By contrast, he accepts the traditional doctrine that sees in might the legitimate basis for authority, "for the sword," he says, "gives a veritable right" (119). This right is conferred by the possession of might. Pascal's formula recalls the axiom of the French monarchy, of feudal origin: "The king depends only on God and his sword." This meant that the Frankish kings depended neither on the pope nor on the emperor; they ensured by force of arms that the justice owed them was duly rendered.

From this Pascal draws an argument for maintaining the order of the world: "Otherwise one would see violence on one side and justice on the other. / End of the 12th *Provincial Letter*" (119). The use of force is not unjust since it allows justice and violence to find themselves on the same side; it allows violence to be legitimate, whereas an overly literal interpretation of justice would become un-just. "An extreme in law is an extreme injustice," Pascal recalls, citing Cicero's adage: "*Summum jus, summa injuria*" (119).

Pascal's reference here to the twelfth *Provincial Letter* attests to the continuity between the *Letters* against the Jesuits and the *Pensées.* In the conflict that pitted Port-Royal against the ecclesias-tical authorities, might and justice did not find themselves on the same side:

> You think you have power and impunity on your side, but I think I have truth and innocence on mine. It is a long strange war when violence tries to suppress truth. All the efforts of violence cannot weaken truth, and only serve to reinforce it. (*PL* 12, pp. 191–192)

Between violence and truth, the contradiction is absolute, insol-uble. Pascal, as usual, explores all the possible outcomes the com-bination offers:

> When power fights power, the greater destroys the less; when ar-gument is set against argument, those which are true and con-vincing confound and disperse those which are only vanity and lies; but violence and truth have no power over each other. (*PL* 12, p. 192)

Violence and truth belong to two different orders. A constraint exercised by one order on another is tyranny. But truth will always win out:

> Let no one claim, however, that they are equal; for there is the enormous difference that the course of violence is limited by the decree of God, who consigns its effects to the glory of the

truth it attacks, whereas truth exists eternally and finally triumphs over its enemies, because it is eternal and mighty as God himself. (*PL* 12, p. 192)

If justice and might do not find themselves on the same side, then truth is on one side and might on the other. And might becomes violent and tyrannical: this amounts to saying that it loses its legitimacy, and it confirms that Pascal has encountered tyranny in the church and not in the state—the tyranny of the pope and the bishops: "Justice without might is impotent. Might without justice is tyrannical," as we read in the *Pensées* as well (135).

In Pascal's eyes, Port-Royal, which defended the doctrine of efficacious grace and predestination, was on the side of truth. By contrast, the Jesuits, who supported the thesis of sufficient grace and free will, had might on their side.

In 1661, when the Sisters of Port-Royal, among them Jacqueline Pascal, who had become Sister Jacqueline de Sainte-Euphrémie, were required by Alexander the Seventh to sign an oath condemning Jansen's five propositions, they had truth on their side, whereas the archbishop of Paris had the power to constrain on his side and committed violence. Jacqueline, opposed to signing, at first refused to compromise. One turn of phrase in a letter she wrote to Antoine Arnauld showed that while she had buried her poetic talent, she had not lost her style: "Since the bishops have the courage of girls, girls must have the courage of bishops" (*OC* 4:1086). She nevertheless elected to sign in June 1661, and she died shortly afterward, in October, a victim of violence exercised against the truth.

16

"Greatness of Establishment, Respect of Establishment"

Here is a very elliptical but crucial fragment of the *Pensées:* "Greatness of establishment, respect of establishment" (650).

An establishment is a constituted body, a stable institution, an imposing state. In establishments there is might, authority, rank. Before an establishment, one bows, one shows respect.

By "greatness of establishment," an expression that is his own, Pascal refers to the status granted to a man by virtue of his birth, his social position, and his official status, and respect of establishment is owed to the man or woman (but generally a man) who enjoys such greatness. Under the old regime, it was the respect shown by members of the third estate to nobles and clergy, to people of rank and distinction.

In the letter dedicating his arithmetic machine to Chancellor Séguier, in 1645, Pascal addressed the recipient as "Your Greatness"

(*OC* 2:331–334). Tallemant des Réaux, who disliked Séguier, pointed out that the latter coveted praise and was the first chancellor to bestow on himself the title of Greatness.

Pascal's reflection on the "greatness of establishment" is amplified in the second of three "Discourses on the Condition of the Greats," a set of political reflections. Pascal did not compose these himself, but his friend Pierre Nicole published them in 1670 in a treatise called "On the Education of a Prince." In the *Pensées,* the fragments that announced these "discourses" can be dated to the summer of 1660. Nicole is thought to have faithfully transcribed the lessons Pascal gave the young duc de Chevreuse, the son of the duc de Luynes, who was closely associated with Port-Royal: "There are, in the world, two sorts of greatness; for there is greatness of establishment and natural greatness. Greatness of establishment depends on the will of men, who have believed rightly that they must honor certain statuses and accord certain respects to them" (*OC* 4:1032).

In France, one honors birth, rank, and age. This is arbitrary. One does so "because it has pleased men" to do so, and "the thing was indifferent before its establishment." Still, "after establishment, it becomes just, because it is unjust to disturb it"; such a disturbance would upset public order. Let us thus bow before the established greats.

In contrast with "grandeurs of establishment," Pascal identifies "natural greatnesses." Natural greatnesses are not arbitrary but rather

> independent of human fantasies, because they consist in real
> and effective qualities of the soul or the body, which make the

one or the other more estimable, such as knowledge, intelligence, virtue, health, strength. (*OC* 4:1032)

Natural grandeur is that of the body or the soul, that of an athlete, a scholar, or a wise man. Pascal recognizes both sorts, but he emphasizes their difference:

> To grandeurs of establishment, we owe the respects of establishment, that is, certain external ceremonies . . . , but which do not make us conceive of some real quality in those whom we honor this way. . . . As for the forms of natural respect that consist in esteem, we owe them only to natural greatnesses. (*OC* 4:1032)

I must bow to a duke because he is a duke, and I must think that that is just, but I can excuse myself from esteeming him if he does not deserve my esteem. The duties that one renders to greatnesses of establishment are "external duties," and these can coexist with what Pascal calls the "inner scorn" that a great man sometimes deserves owing to the baseness of his mind.

The distinction between the two greatnesses had already been suggested in 1652, in Pascal's letter to Queen Christina of Sweden, written when he was presenting her with his arithmetic machine:

> I have a quite special veneration for those who have risen to the supreme degree either of power or of knowledge. The latter, if I am not mistaken, can pass for sovereigns just as much as the former. (*OC* 2:924)

Pascal admired the princes of the mind, the intellectual aristocracy to which he flattered himself that he belonged, before he converted to humility: "Each of these empires is great in itself"

(*OC* 2:924), but intellectual greatness wins out in glory, in his eyes, over the aristocracy of birth. The friendship between Pascal and the duc de Roannez, between a noble and a scholar, was all the more sincere in that the duke was also a prince of the mind.

Justice, which is essential for social order, requires respect for the greatnesses of establishment. But Pascal, with his combinatory turn of mind, explores all the possibilities: just as it would be unjust to render natural respect to greatness of establishment, it would be unjust to render respect of establishment to natural greatness—for example, to allow a scholar to take precedence over me on the pretext that he is a scholar if I am superior to him by virtue of my status. I can recognize him as more knowledgeable than myself, but I must come before him.

In short, to greatness of establishment belongs respect of establishment and to natural greatness, natural esteem. Let us not mix the orders. Let us not doff our hats to a scholar, and above all let us not give our esteem to a "great man" who does not deserve it; let us settle for bowing before him. And let us not forget that Pascal converses with the son of a duke and teaches him lessons, so that he will later deserve both his teacher's respect and his esteem.

17

"*Thought Escaped*"

There is a whole art of thinking, an art of writing, an art of reading, to be discovered in the *Pensées*. On the margins of anthropology and theology are hidden a number of little reflections to which we moderns may be sensitive:

> To understand the meaning of an author, one must reconcile all the contradictory passages. . . . Every author has a meaning with which all the contradictory passages are in harmony, or he has no meaning at all. (289)

This fragment is titled "Contradiction," and Pascal is thinking above all of the Bible and its numerous "contradictory passages," which can scandalize libertines. He reminds us of an ancient hermeneutic or interpretive principle that was followed by the fathers of the church, Saint Augustine in particular. It is a matter of reconciling contradictions, for, as Pascal says, "in Jesus Christ all contradictions are resolved." Pascal, with his geometric mind, doesn't hesitate to apply a hermeneutic rule of coherence that is valid for all authors and all books, including Scripture.

Elsewhere, we are stopped short by this outburst: "Thought escaped, I wanted to write it: I write instead that it has escaped me" (459).

Roland Barthes cites this sentence several times; he sees it as a good example of the new discipline he would like to invent, *bathmology,* or the "study of degrees of language": instead of writing the forgotten thought, I move up a degree and write that I have forgotten it.

Pascal's reflection comes after this remark: "Chance gives thoughts, and chance takes them away; hardly an art for preserving or for acquiring."

The art of acquiring and preserving thoughts: we recognize the components of the old rhetoric, *inventio* and *memoria.* The scientific method of the sixteenth and seventeenth centuries broke with the art of memory that had been taught from antiquity through the Renaissance. The art of memory boasted that it could produce new knowledge, form new thoughts by recombining ideas. Science condemned the hermeneutic speculations of the artisans of memory and refuted the artificial rhetorical techniques that made it possible not to forget one's thoughts: "True eloquence cares little for eloquence," and orators would no longer run through an architecture of memory to recover in each room the ideas and words they had placed there.

In addition, deep truths do not reside in memory but in the heart, which does not forget. If a thought has escaped, it is because it was not essential but random; it was a false good idea.

> As I write down my thought, it sometimes escapes me, but that makes me remember my weakness, which I am constantly forgetting. This instructs me as much as my forgotten thought, for I cling only to the knowledge of my nothingness. (540)

A good idea comes to mind, shaped in a good formula, that I would like to write down in my notebook. However, just as I was about to record it, it went out of my head. Forgetting it nevertheless aroused another thought, a much more important one: the recognition of my wretchedness, my weakness, or my nothingness, which I am precisely trying to forget. The experience of forgetting the thought gives rise to a thought about forgetting, through a sort of reflexive activity—or, in modern terms, self-referentiality.

Pascal's memory, however, was legendary. He knew the Bible, "almost all of it by heart," Gilberte reports (*OC* 1:582), and "he himself said that he had never forgotten anything he had wanted to retain," according to his niece Marguerite Périer (*OC* 1:1103), or anything "he had at one point understood by reason," according to his friend Pierre Nicole (*OC* 1:987). The escaped thought was thus nonessential.

In view of his apologia and despite his good memory, Pascal noted his thoughts on large sheets of paper, in disorder, randomly, as they came to him. Later, he cut them into strips and categorized them, and this is how the *Pensées* are presented, as a more or less ordered memory aid. The fragments that he placed as headings sketch out an overall plan in two parts (after *inventio* comes *dispositio,* the order of discourse): "First Part: Wretchedness of Man without God. / Second Part: Felicity of Man with God" (40).

The gentlemen of Port-Royal, disappointed by this disorder, ended up publishing them under the simple title *Pensées,* but certain editors are still trying to reconstitute the exact arrangement of the apologia conceived by Pascal. It's a lost cause. The result of Pascal's genius, along with his poor health, was that he launched into numerous extraordinary projects but completed virtually none. And he said: "The last thing one finds in making a work is knowing what should come first" (740).

So we have to settle for the imperfect copies of the *Pensées* produced after his death.

18

"He Is Neither Angel nor Beast, but Man"

"Man must not believe that he is equal to beasts or angels, nor should he remain ignorant of either, but he must know both" (154).

Pascal begins his apologia by humiliating human beings, degrading them, plunging them into their wretchedness. But this is not the last word. Humans are intermediate creatures, divided between wretchedness and greatness. After showing them the evidence of their wretchedness, one must also make them aware of the remnants of their greatness. That way they will know their condition as a whole.

Once again Pascal proves faithful to Saint Augustine, for whom *Medius homo est inferior angelis, superior pecoribus:* "Thus man is an intermediate being, but intermediate between beasts or angels," angels themselves being intermediaries between man and God (*Concerning the City of God,* bk. 9, chap. 13, p. 1044).

Montaigne, whom Pascal has at his fingertips, wrote in the final chapter of the *Essays,* "Of Experience": "They want to get out of themselves and escape from the man. That is madness: instead of changing into angels, they change into beasts; instead of raising themselves, they lower themselves" (bk. 3, chap. 13, p. 856).

Man is not at the same time both angel and beast; he is neither the one nor the other, but he can make himself equivalent to one or the other or take himself for the one or the other.

Here we find the two philosophical schools or sects on which Pascal bases his whole demonstration: the Stoics, represented by Epictetus, and the Pyrrhonians, or Skeptics, represented by Montaigne. The controversy reported in the "Conversation with M. de Sacy about Epictetus and Montaigne," which was supposed to have taken place in 1658, around the time Pascal is thought to have presented the outline of his apology to his friends at Port-Royal, was the real premise of the *Pensées*.

Pride characterizes the Stoics, who think they can make themselves equal to the angels; indolence or lowliness characterizes the Pyrrhonians, as well as the Epicureans and probably the libertines, who see themselves as equals to beasts: "The ones sought to renounce the passions and become gods; the others sought to renounce reason and become brute beasts" (29).

But members of neither camp have managed to rid themselves either of passions or of reason. For man is irremediably intermediate.

We must not be surprised, Pascal also says, to see a man who has just lost his wife and his only son engaging in diversions such as gambling or hunting, "occupied and full of concern with taking a hare," for "he is only a man, in the end, that is, capable of little and much, of everything and nothing" (453). The important word here is "capable," capable of little but also of much, of nothing but also of everything.

Pascal condemns man but also elevates him, for in man there remain traces of his original nature:

> The greatness of man is great in that he knows he is wretched. / A tree does not know it is wretched. One experiences wretchedness in knowing that one is wretched, but one experiences greatness in knowing that one is wretched. (146)

Let us go further: the two contradictory options, angel and beast, Stoicism and Pyrrhonism, amount to the same thing. Pascal has more than one dialectical trick in his bag, more than one way of shifting between pros and cons and surpassing them both: "Man is neither angel nor beast, and whoever wants to act the angel acts the beast" (557).

This thought strikes with the memorable force of a moral maxim, and it has been received as such: the proud will be brought down; a fall is the just punishment for pride.

But in the *Pensées* this proposition has a theological meaning above all: seeking to be an angel is to lay claim to a superior nature in the hierarchy of beings. By his presumption, a man who is unaware of original sin distances himself all the further from God, and this degrades him further, bringing him closer to beasts. If man fails to know his wretchedness, neglects the contrariness of his dual nature, and recognizes only his greatness, he becomes even more wretched. Thus, exempting himself from the domination of God, "today man has become like the beasts" (182). The other branch of the alternative is no better, for the Pyrrhonians and the Epicureans,

> who saw the vanity of that pretention have thrust you into the other precipice, by giving you to understand that your nature was

like that of the beasts, and they have led you to seek your good in
the concupiscence that is the animals' lot. (182)

The only way out for man consists in recognizing both his
wretchedness and his greatness, the contradiction that defines
his nature, in the tradition of Nicholas de Cues's *coincidentia op-
positorum,* or "coincidence of opposites." As Pascal reminds us: "At
the end of every truth, we must add that we remember the opposite truth" (479).

19

The Libertines

The "Apology for the Christian Religion" has a single purpose: to convert its readers, who are interlocutors rather than adversaries. The intended recipients are the libertines (even though the word does not appear in the *Pensées*) who made up the circle of friends Pascal frequented during his so-called worldly period, such as the chevalier de Méré or Damien Mitton (mentioned three times in the *Pensées*). Pascal uses ad hominem arguments: he starts from hypotheses accepted by the libertines in order to lead them to conclusions they initially had rejected.

But we need to be careful here! A libertine in Pascal's day was not, as is the case today, someone of loose morals; he was someone whose thought was unfettered, who exercised his thinking apart from any dogmatic constraints: he was a free thinker, a deist, an atheist, or a person characterized by indifference to religion. For such a person, the first among liberties was freedom of conscience, independence of thought with respect to Christian religion and morality.

Méré and Mitton were worldly men, gentlemen, practitioners and also theoreticians of *honnêteté*—that is, of the art of being happy and making those around you happy. They shared with Pascal this premise of the *Pensées:* "We seek happiness" (20).

Pascal took little interest in the other side of libertinage, the scholarly side that was more threatening to dogma. Deploying a critical spirit in the name of history and philosophy, erudite thinkers such as Pietro Pomponazzi and Gabriel Naudé challenged the verities of Christianity, such as the Incarnation, the Trinity, and the Eucharist. In the *Pensées,* Pascal makes passing reference to the hypothesis of the pre-Adamites (478) and to Chinese chronology (663); he alludes to the contradictions in the Gospels concerning Christ's genealogy (268) and summarizes the atheists' objections:

> What reason do they have for saying that one cannot resuscitate? Which is harder, to be born or to resuscitate? That something that has never been, exists, or that something that has been, exists again? Is it harder to come into being than to return to it? Custom makes one easy, the lack of custom makes the other impossible. Popular way of judging. / Why can't a virgin give birth? Doesn't a hen lay eggs without a rooster? And who told us that the hen cannot form that seed as well as the rooster? (444)

His discussion with his worldly interlocutors is much more concise: "The self is hateful. You, Mitton, cover it up, you do not thereby rid yourself of it. You are thus still hateful" (494).

Here Pascal is sketching an imaginary dialogue with his freethinking friend. He reproaches Mitton for not truly renouncing self-love, for simply cloaking it in altruism. *Honnêteté* of course forbids putting one's self on display, but it cannot neutralize the injurious effects of egoism.

The dialogue goes on, and Mitton replies: "No, for in acting as we do, obligingly toward everyone, we leave you no reason to hate us." But this defense is not enough for Pascal:

> That is true, if one hates in the self only the displeasure that it brings us. But if I hate someone because it is unjust that he makes himself the center of everything, I shall always hate him. (494)

Even if the honnête libertine's self is not tyrannical and does not seek to subjugate others, it remains unjust, thus hateful, because it is unaware that self-love results from original sin and can only be eradicated by Christian virtue. "Mitton sees very well that nature is corrupt and that men are opposed to honnêteté," Pascal adds. "But he does not know why they cannot fly higher" (529 *bis*).

Men cannot fly higher because they are not angels but fallen creatures: "The heart of man is hollow and full of filth" (171), Pascal makes clear, and honnêteté cannot change this; only God can.

"Reproach Mitton for not bestirring himself" (433). This is the whole aim of the apology: the point is to oblige Mitton to take action, to shake up the libertine honnête homme, the impious but in no way debauched atheist. Pascal addresses him here in a language quite different from that of the *Provincial Letters,* which is studded with quotations from casuists. Here, Pascal is speaking in his interlocutor's own language, that of a libertine honnête homme, a language that has ensured the success of the *Pensées* over more than three centuries despite Port-Royal's scorn for this pile of first drafts.

20

"Joy, Joy, Joy, Tears of Joy"

After Pascal's death, a domestic servant found, sewn into the lining of his doublet, a carefully folded parchment, which he gave to Gilberte. The family understood that "this parchment, written with so much care and with such remarkable lettering," was a "sort of memorial" that Pascal always kept close at hand; it related a spiritual experience that took place the night of November 23, 1654 (*OC* 3:56). What had happened to him? A vision, an apparition, a rapture, a mystical ecstasy? We must be prudent in using such words. But his definitive conversion to Port-Royal followed.

After his father's death, the letter of consolation Pascal wrote in October 1651 to his sister Gilberte and his brother-in-law already bore evidence of his familiarity with Augustinian thought. His sister Jacqueline had left him in January 1652 to become a nun at Port-Royal. During the next two years, Pascal spent time with the duc de Roannez and the libertines Méré and Mitton, and he pursued various projects in physics and mathematics that included the invention of the "geometry of chance" to solve the problem of gambling odds that interested his friend Méré. However, Jacqueline dated the beginning of her brother's detachment from the world to the fall of 1653. On December 8, 1654, she confided in a letter to Gilberte: "It is not reasonable that you should remain unaware any longer of what God is undertaking in the person who is so dear to us"; that person has had "for more than a year now great contempt for the world and an almost unbearable disgust for everyone who is part of it" (*OC* 3:67–68).

Then the conversion sped up. Jacqueline wrote to her brother, rather bluntly, on January 19, 1655: "I am astonished that God has given you that grace, for it seems to me that you had deserved in many ways to be bothered for some time more by the stench of the quagmire you had embraced with such eagerness" (*OC* 3:69).

Then, in a letter to Gilberte dated January 25, 1655, Jacqueline related a visit her brother had made in September 1654: "He opened up to me in a way that made me feel pity, by confessing that amidst his great projects and all the things that could help make him love the world, and to which there was reason to believe him strongly attached, he was being called to abandon it all in such a way that, through the extreme aversion he had to the follies and amusements of the world and through the constant reproach his conscience addressed to him, he found himself detached from all things in a way he never had been before, not in the slightest; but that moreover he was in such a great abandonment on God's side that he felt no attraction in that direction" (*OC* 3:71).

Disgusted with the world, he felt at once unattracted and abandoned by God. The resolution came about abruptly, the absence of

God leaving space for the fire of the presence of a God understood with the heart.

Jacqueline and Gilberte took note of their brother's conversion, but the event of November 23, 1654, remained a secret. They knew nothing of the "night of fire" that had marked the end of Pascal's worldly life, of his project of marrying and taking on official responsibilities, of his dreams of scientific glory, nor of his "delicious and criminal use of the world," as he put it in 1660 in his "Prayer to Ask God for the Good Use of Illnesses" (*OC* 4:999).

This conversion, which had nothing to do with the wager, resembles a spiritual experience, followed by a meditation. In the eighteenth century, the rationalists would see it as hallucinatory, and Condorcet characterized it as "madness," but the lexicon of the "Memorial" reflects peace, joy, and sweetness (742):

> From about half past ten in the evening until about half past midnight.
>
> Fire
>
> . . . Certainty, certainty, feeling, joy, peace.

Following the mysterious phenomenon that "Fire" seems to designate, comfort wins out over terror and anguish.

> Forgotten, the world and everything, apart from God.
> He is found only through the paths taught in the Gospel.
> Greatness of the human soul.
> Just Father, the world has not known you, but I have known you.
> Joy, joy, joy, tears of joy!

And to conclude: "Total, sweet renunciation."

The "Memorial" expresses certainty, trust, tenderness, and consolation, the absent God making his presence felt in the writer's
heart. Some commentators prefer to see it as an ascetic rather than
a mystical experience. The "Memorial" contains several biblical
quotations, with the Fire manifesting itself simultaneously to the
heart and the mind, not dismissing reason.

But joy dominates. It confirms that the terror and anguish that
reign in the *Pensées* stem more from dramatization than from self-
portraiture and aim indeed to confound the libertines.

21

Pascal's Method

Pascal's method is pretty much always the same. He presents two opposing theses, shows that they are both false, and proposes a third that surpasses them both by combining them, keeping what was right in each and discarding what was wrong. Or else, more paradoxically and even more forcefully, he asserts that the opposing theses are both correct, and he maintains them both by invoking the coincidence of opposites.

The procedure was perfected in his "Writings on Grace," the key to the *Provincial Letters* and the *Pensées* alike.

On one side, the Calvinists claimed that it was the will of God, in creating men, to save some of them and condemn others before anticipating any merit or demerit: this is absolute predestination. On the other side, the Jesuits, or Molinists, argued that God wanted, equally, generally, but conditionally, to save all men, as long as they wanted to be saved; he left it up to their free will to decide whether or not they wanted salvation by means of the sufficient grace He gave all men (*OC* 3:766).

Pascal deemed the Calvinists' position atrocious and intolerable, for it presupposed a cruel God; he found the Molinists' position gentle, agreeable, and charming, for it supposes free men. But for him, both positions were excessive and false. Between the two, and combining them, the correct opinion was Saint Augustine's,

> neither as cruel as Calvin's nor as gentle as Molina's. . . . The Molinists claim that predestination and reprobation come from the forecasting of men's merits and sins. / The Calvinists claim that predestination and reprobation come from the absolute will of God. And the Church claims that predestination comes from the will of God and reprobation from the forecasting of sin. (*OC* 3:767–768)

In addition, "the Molinists posit the will of men as the source of salvation and damnation," "the Calvinists posit the will of God as the source of salvation and damnation," and "the Church posits that the will of God is the source of salvation, and that the will of men is the source of damnation" (*OC* 3:767–768).

Thus, the true Augustinian doctrine of grace, followed by the Jansenists, is presented as a coincidence of two opposing truths: we are predestined, we are free. But isn't this solution, which has logic and mystery on its side, somewhat sophistic, or even casuistic? And hasn't Pascal succeeded in establishing that the Port-Royal thesis is identical to church dogma?

He uses an analogous procedure with regard to natural philosophy in the "Conversation with M. de Sacy about Epictetus and Montaigne," "the two most illustrious defenders of the two most celebrated sects in the world" (*OC* 3:151). On one side, Epictetus and the Stoics insist on man's greatness; on the other, Montaigne and the Skeptics, or Pyrrhonians, show man's weakness. One school is characterized by presumption; the other, by doubt that leads to nonchalance. To get out of the impasse, Pascal takes both positions apart and retains what is good in each:

> The source of the errors of these two sects is not having known that the state of man at present differs from that of his creation, such that one of them, noticing some traces of man's initial greatness, and unaware of his corruption, has treated nature as healthy and not in need of a savior, which leads him to the pinnacle of arrogance. Meanwhile, the other, experiencing man's present wretchedness and not knowing his initial dignity, treats nature as necessarily infirm and irreparable, plunging him into despair of reaching true goodness, and from there into extreme indolence. Thus these two states, which one needed to grasp together in order to see the whole truth, were grasped separately, leading necessarily to one of two vices, pride and sloth, conditions sure to affect all men who lack grace, since, if they do not remain in their disorders by dint of indolence, they get out of them by dint of vanity. (*OC* 3:152)

By combining the greatness of man recognized by one side and the wretchedness exposed by the other, one can avoid both pride and indolence:

> From these imperfect insights it thus happens that one of them, knowing man's duties and unaware of his impotence, gets lost in presumption, and the other, knowing impotence and not duty, lapses into indolence. (*OC* 3:153)

There is no better initiation to the method that will be used in the *Pensées,* and to the dual condition of man, than placing Stoics and Skeptics back to back:

> Know then, arrogant one, what a paradox you are for yourself! Humble yourself, impotent reason! Keep still, imbecilic nature! Learn that man infinitely transcends man and learn from your Master your true condition, of which you are ignorant. / Listen to God. (164)

There is no finer dialectic: we can understand why Marxists have admired it.

22

The "Sublime Misanthropist"

The Enlightenment thinkers were embarrassed by Pascal. On the one hand, they respected the scientific genius who had proved the existence of the vacuum and invented the calculus of probabilities. On the other hand, they condemned the sanctimonious retrograde who had believed in miracles, theorized the necessity of efficacious grace, and defended the rigoristic morality of Port-Royal. They resolved the contradiction with the hypothesis that he had gone mad.

Voltaire wrote to a friend: "Pascal always thought he saw an abyss beside his chair: must we for that reason imagine as much? . . . Toward the end, melancholy led Pascal's reason astray. . . . It is not astonishing, after all, that a man of delicate temperament, with a sorrowful imagination, like Pascal, should have managed, owing to a poor diet, to disrupt the organs of his brain" (*Lettre à M. de's Gravesande,* June 1, 1741). But the legend of the abyss that Pascal was said to have pictured at his left was not mentioned before 1737, long after his death (*OC* 1:969).

The free thinkers of the eighteenth century based their views on a trauma that Pascal was thought to have suffered after a carriage accident on the Neuilly bridge, in which the horses had bitten through the brakes and plunged into the Seine, leaving the carriage suspended over the void; a terrified Pascal would have seen his death at hand. According to this account, the mental disorder that followed led to the vision of the "night of fire" and convinced Pascal to "live in complete solitude" (*OC* 1:885). But this account appears, conveniently, only in 1740.

For Condorcet, a number of the collected fragments in the *Pensées* are marked by misguided reasoning or even dementia. Having given up physics and mathematics, Pascal was said to have become a visionary. And Voltaire wrote to Condorcet in 1776: "So that Blaise touched at once on extreme mental power and extreme madness? This is good to know; one can draw strange conclusions from it." As early as 1734, in his *Philosophical Letters* Voltaire had asserted: "I venture to take the side of humanity against this sublime misanthropist" (letter 25, p. 119).

The abyss and the accident in Neuilly made it possible to save the man of science and to condemn the believer. Condorcet, in his 1776 edition of the *Pensées,* went so far as to characterize the "Memorial," which appeared for the first time in 1740, as a "mystical amulet."

Gilberte Périer's "Life" of her brother had contributed to the legend of his declining health: "He had, among other afflictions, that of being unable to swallow liquids unless they were hot; and even then he could only do it drop by drop. . . . Beyond that, he had an unbearable headache, excessive intestinal burning, and many other ailments" (*OC* 1:581).

Marguerite Périer, his niece, completed the myth in her own "Memoir" dating from the early eighteenth century. During his second year of life, she related, Pascal was gravely ill: he couldn't bear to see water or to see his father and his mother near each other; then he fell into a "languor similar to what is called in Paris wasting away"—so much so that one night he was thought to have died. A spell was said to have been cast on him by a woman who frequented the house and who agreed, under pressure from Étienne Pascal, to shift the spell onto a cat. The anecdote is surprising: Blaise's father was a legal scholar and a mathematician, a reasonable man. If the story is true, science and superstition coexisted in that enlightened person (*OC* 1:1091–1093).

We do not know for sure which illness, cancer or tuberculosis, took Pascal's life at the age of thirty-nine, or Jacqueline's at age thirty-six. After the Enlightenment, the figure of the sick genius, suffering, in pain, tragic, was rehabilitated by Romanticism. Only Sainte-Beuve, a free-thinking rationalist, doubted the effect of illness on Pascal's scientific and literary work: "Without claiming to deny Pascal's singular nervous accidents, and their impact on his mood or his thinking, we maintain that from this distance, and according to the information transmitted, there is no evidence on which to base any *diagnostic,* as they say. What strikes us, on the contrary, as positive, is that, however much he may be seen as suffering from a nervous condition, Pascal retained to the end the integrity of his moral conscience and his understanding. The rest escapes us" (*Port-Royal* 2:332).

However, Sainte-Beuve maintained the same skepticism as Voltaire and Condorcet regarding the miracle of the Holy Thorn said to have cured Marguerite Périer and vindicated Port-Royal in 1656 and thereafter to have spawned the initial project of the *Pensées* as a treatise on miracles.

23

"A King without Diversions"

"Diversion" (*divertissement*) is one of the key notions of the anthropology Pascal set forth at the beginning of the *Pensées*. The word does not have its modern, banal sense of leisure, activities practiced in one's free time, or entertainment. Instead, it has a much more serious—and paradoxical—meaning, as is often the case in Pascal: diversion is for humankind the means of turning away, diverting oneself in the literal sense from the misery of life, a means of concealing from oneself the vanity of the human condition, a means of refusing to acknowledge "ennui" (irritation, trouble)[1] and "inquietude" (uneasiness, anxiety), two very strong terms to be understood as profound anguish. Diversion is everything that impedes the search for the truth of God, and if Pascal insists so strongly on the point, it is because

---

1. In seventeenth-century French, the word "ennui" lacked the connotations of listlessness and boredom that it has taken on in contemporary English. In contemporary French, the primary meaning is something like dissatisfaction, annoyance at some obstacle or difficulty.

he has to overturn the obstacle that diversion presents to his planned apologia.

"As men have not been able to cure death, misery, ignorance, to make themselves happy they have decided not to think at all" (166), he proclaims in one fragment of the "Diversion" sheaf of the *Pensées*. And in another: "A king without diversions is a man full of miseries" (169); Jean Giono was to make this the title of one of his best novels (*Un roi sans divertissement,* translated as *Second Harvest*). Diversions allow us to blind ourselves to the world, which Pascal depicts as a prison, a terrifying cell that we want to flee. Here is the paradox:

> When I have sometimes set out to consider the various agitations of men and the perils and the pains to which they expose themselves at Court, in war, which gives rise to so many quarrels, passions, bold and often misguided ventures, etc., I have often said that all the unhappiness of mankind comes from just one thing, which is not knowing how to remain at rest in a room. (168)

Yes, how lovely it would be to withdraw, to stop, to rest! This was the ideal of the ancient wisdom. But no, our "thoughts in the back of the mind" remind us that there is nothing better than a vacation or retreat to give us migraines and provoke distress. As soon as we stop what we are doing, we are confronted with our own condition.

> When I gave the matter closer thought and after having found the cause of all our unhappiness I wanted to find the reason for it, I found that there is indeed a very real one that consists in the natural unhappiness of our weak, mortal condition, so wretched that nothing can console us when we think about it closely. (168)

So we bustle about. Pascal proceeds yet again via the "cause of effects": the first explanation of the moralist was too brief; withdrawal does not procure peace but rather torment instead of the happiness sought; our agitation, on the model of warfare, gambling, or hunting, is explained by the need we feel to escape our fate.

Even a king is not happy:

> If he is without diversions and left to observe and reflect on what he is, this languishing felicity will in no way sustain him. He will necessarily fall into views that threaten him with revolts that may occur, and finally death and illnesses, which are inevitable. So that if he is without what are called diversions, he is unhappy, and more unhappy than the least of his subjects, who plays and entertains himself. (168)

Diversion is universal; it seduces kings and peasants alike:

> From this comes the fact that gambling and conversation with women, war, and high office are so sought after. Not that actual happiness lies there, nor do people imagine that true beatitude lies in having the money one can win by gambling or in the hare one chases after; one wouldn't want to receive such things as gifts. Weak and peaceful practices, which leave us to think about our unhappy condition, are not what we are seeking, nor are the dangers of war or the pain of work; it is rather the commotion that distracts and diverts us from such thoughts. (168)

Thus, diversions are by no means absurd; they are even reasonable, for without them life would be unbearable. But they must be endlessly renewed.

Look at "that man, who recently lost his only son and who, bur-
dened with trials and quarrels, was so troubled this morning" but
who "is no longer thinking about that now"; the reason is that he

> is fully occupied in seeing where that wild boar will go, the one
> the dogs have been pursuing so ardently for six hours. It doesn't
> take more than this. The man, however full of sorrow he may be,
> if one can prevail on him to enter into some diversion, will be
> happy during that time. . . . Without diversion there is no joy.
> With diversion there is no sorrow. (168; cf. 453)

Voltaire, in his *Philosophical Letters,* does not pass negative judgment on that man, who "does very well." Whether he knows it or
not, "dissipation is a better cure for sorrow than quinine is for fever;
then let us not accuse nature, which is always ready to rescue us"
(letter 25, p. 113).

24

The Three Orders

Pascal likes distinctions, categorizations, gradations. In the letter to Queen Christina of Sweden in 1652 that accompanied the gift of his arithmetic machine, he distinguishes two orders in the world, that of bodies and that of minds. There are sovereigns in the order of bodies, the men and women who exercise power, and there are sovereigns in the order of minds, the men and women of science. But "minds are of a higher order than bodies," and "in [her] sacred person" Christina of Sweden unites "sovereign authority and solid science" (*OC* 2:924).

In the *Pensées,* the orders are three in number: bodies, minds, and charity—in other words, the material or fleshly order, the intellectual order, and the spiritual order. According to Jean Mesnard, this triad is the basis for Pascal's thought.

The infinite distance from bodies to minds figures the infinitely more infinite distance between minds and charity, for the latter is supernatural. / All the glow of greatness has no luster for people

who are pursuing quests of the mind. / The greatness of intellect
is invisible to kings, to the rich, to captains, to all these bodily
greats. The greatness of wisdom, which is nothing without God,
is invisible to the sensual and the intellectual alike. These are three
different kinds of orders. (339)

Thus, there are in the world three orders of things that cannot be
reduced or conflated. The order of the flesh includes all forms of
might: the great figures of flesh are princes, warlords, the wealthy.
Scientists, inventors, and creators belong to the order of the mind;
Pascal offers Archimedes as the model. The order of charity, finally, is
that of God. From one order to the next, the gap is insurmountable:
those who are great in the order of the mind are indifferent to the
greatnesses of the flesh and vice versa. And man has no access
through his natural forces to the third order, that of charity.

The great geniuses have their empire, their brilliance, their greatness, their victories and their luster, and they have no need of
fleshly greatness, with which they have no relations. They are seen
not by eyes but by minds. That is enough. / The saints have their
empires, their brilliance, their victories, their luster, and have no
need of fleshly greatnesses or of those of the mind, with which
they have no relations. They are seen by God and the angels and
not by bodies or curious minds. God is enough for them. (339)

Among the three orders, the separation and disproportion are
absolute: the greatness of one order means nothing to the higher
order, persons of a lower order can understand nothing about the
higher order, and the distance is "infinitely infinite" between
the first two (the flesh and the mind) and the third (charity).

But the three orders have the same structure, and each has its greatness. Thus, the lower orders, while unable to understand the higher orders or to provide access to them, can nevertheless give an idea of the higher orders: bodies can respect minds, and minds can conceive, however slightly, of what belongs to charity. The distance between bodies and minds, Pascal says, "figures" the distance between minds and charity. The term "figure" is important: it is used both in a geometric sense and a theological sense. Many fragments in the theological portion of the *Pensées* are titled "Figures," and many of them are found together in the sheaf labeled "That the Law Was Figurative," bearing on the Old and New Testaments. The distance between bodies and minds is "figurative" of the distance between minds and charity, just as the Old Testament announces the New and even though this second distance is "infinitely more infinite" than the first.

Finally, three forms of faith—of the body, of the mind, and of charity—correspond to those three orders, but only the last one is inspired:

> There are three ways to believe: reason, custom, and inspiration. The Christian religion, which alone has reason, does not acknowledge as its true children those who believe without inspiration. It is not that it excludes reason and custom, on the contrary, but one must open one's mind to the proofs, confirm them by habit, but offer oneself to inspiration by practicing humility, which alone can produce the true and salutary effect. (655)

The first two paths toward conversion—custom and reason—are natural paths that man can take on his own. But these are secondary causes. Inspiration by way of grace is the primary cause, the internal movement of the heart toward faith, and this cause is supernatural.

Even if the orders have no common measure, for Pascal it remains essential to maintain a figurative relation among them. If the distance between body and mind were not in some way able to figure the distance between mind and charity, the project of an apologia for religion addressed to libertines would be vain.

25

"*The Heart Has Its Reasons*"

"The heart has its reasons, which reason does not know" (680). Who has not heard this very well-balanced sentence? It figures in the margins of Pascal's writing on the wager and contradicts the calculation presented there, as a note on the same piece of paper indicates: "It is the heart that feels God and not reason; this is what faith is. God perceptible to the heart, not to reason" (680).

The wager, which appeals to reason, cannot do very much if the heart is not touched by grace.

Reason and the heart: here is another of the essential distinctions that Pascal gradually refines. In "On the Art of Persuasion" we have seen the pairing of understanding and will as the two means by which natural truths can penetrate the soul. But divine truths, Pascal added, enter the soul through the grace of God, "from the heart into the mind, and not from the mind into the heart" (*OC* 3:413). We are to understand that, alongside understanding and will (that is, intellect and desire), there is a place reserved for the heart.

In the *Pensées,* the faculties are organized somewhat differently: "We know truth not only through reason but also through the heart; it is via the latter path that we know first principles, and reason, which plays no role here, tries in vain to challenge those principles" (142).

Through the heart, whether by instinct or intuition, we have certainty about the first principles—for example space, time, movement, and numbers. For Pascal the point is to counter the Skeptics and the Pyrrhonians, who doubt everything but do not succeed in making us doubt our own immediate sensations:

> We know that we are not dreaming, however powerless we may
> be to prove this through reason. This powerlessness proves only
> the weakness of our reason, and not the uncertainty of all our
> knowledge, as they claim. (142)

Thus, the heart gives immediate knowledge of the natural truths, and "it is on this knowledge of the heart and the instincts that reason must rely" (142). The heart feels that space has three dimensions and that numbers are infinite, while reason demonstrates that a number squared cannot be the double of another number squared. The heart is a passive faculty, while reason is an active faculty. Consequently, "principles are felt, propositions are proved, and all this with certainty, although by different paths" (142).

But Pascal appeals above all to the heart, which he never defines, to justify faith by grace and to oppose faith to reason: "Knowing God is a far cry from loving him" (409), he declares in a fragment in the last sheaf of the *Pensées*. This sheaf was to have supplied the conclusion of the apologia, at the point where reason must step aside, for it can do no more in the absence of God's grace:

> Those to whom God has given religion through a feeling of the heart are truly happy and very legitimately persuaded. But [to] those who lack it, we cannot give it except by reasoning while waiting for God to bestow it on them through a feeling of their heart. Without which faith is only human and useless for salvation. (142)

The power of the apologist is reduced, but it is not lacking. He cannot inspire faith by a "feeling of the heart," but he can "incline [someone] to seek," as one of the first fragments in the *Pensées* states: "A letter of exhortation to a friend to induce him to seek. And he will reply: 'But of what use will seeking be to me? Nothing is clear.' And to answer him: 'Do not despair.' And he would respond that he would be happy to find some enlightenment, but that according to religion itself, when he would believe in that way, it would be of no use and thus he is just as happy not to seek. And to that, reply: 'The machine'" (39).

"The machine" refers to the bodily practices that induce belief (kneeling, taking holy water). But what will the machine—that is, custom or habit—be able to do? The libertine knows that a simply reasonable and human faith will be of no help to him. For only God puts faith in one's heart, that faith that "makes one say not *Scio* [I know] but *Credo* [I believe]" (41).

It remains the case that "the heart has its reasons," an affirmation that makes it possible even today to contrast Pascal with the

Kantian philosophical tradition—separating "sensitivity" from "understanding"—or with rational choice theory and see him as the precursor of the contemporary theorists of emotions and affects who analyze the role these play in all our judgments and decisions.

26

"It Is Not in Montaigne"

Unlike the purists, Pascal is never afraid of repetition. It occurs, for example, in the following fragment on the collective order that, in the world, results from the aggregation of individual egoisms:

> People have established [*fondé*] and drawn from concupiscence admirable rules for policies, morals, and justice. / But at bottom [*dans le fond*], that ugly underpinning [*fond*] of man, this FIGMENTUM MALUM is only concealed, not removed. (244)

Under the appearance of order, evil remains. And Pascal does not hesitate to repeat himself: in this short passage, the word *fond* appears three times.

Another fragment of the *Pensées* justifies this indifference to repetition:

> When one finds words repeated in a discourse and, in trying to correct them, one finds them so appropriate that changing them would spoil the discourse, one must leave them in; they are the key

> mark. And here we encounter envy, which is blind and does not
> know that this repetition is not a mistake in this place. For there
> is no general rule. (452)

Here the man of science is speaking. If a word is adequate, if it is
appropriate, then the discourse would become less clear if a less appropriate word were substituted for it, and repetition proves to be
better than the artifice of an approximate synonym. Pascal rejects
the general rule that would forbid any repetition and attributes to
envy the reproach that might be addressed to him for a repetition
deemed faulty. It is better to repeat a word than to replace it with a
less apposite one.

Pascal is not Flaubert, obsessed with weeding out repetitions.
Repetitions are indices of his natural style, the mark of a man who
does not hide behind an author:

> When we see natural style, we are wholly astonished and delighted,
> for we were expecting to see an author and we find a man. Un-
> like those who have good taste and who upon seeing a book be-
> lieve they are finding a man and are quite surprised to find an
> author. (554)

And again: "Everything that is only for the author is worthless"
(650).

Because it is precise, the natural style touches the heart:

> When a natural discourse depicts a passion or effect, one finds in
> oneself the truth of what one is hearing, a truth that one did not
> know was there, so that one is led to love the one who makes us
> feel it, for he has not put his own good on display but ours. And

thus this benefit makes him agreeable, beyond the fact that this intellectual bond we have with him necessarily inclines our heart to love him. (536)

The natural style comes across as surpassing of the art of discourse, effacing art in a gradation toward simplicity. It recalls the art of conversation perfected in the salons of the classical era. Following a pedagogy reminiscent of that of Socrates drawing out his questioners' thoughts, the honnête homme seeks not to put his own wit on display but rather to "let the others discover theirs," as La Bruyère would recommend (*Caractères,* chap. 5, p. 130). A discourse will be more effective if it allows the interlocutor to form his own ideas, draw his own conclusions, for, according to Pascal, "one is usually better persuaded by the reasons one has found oneself than by those that came into the minds of others" (617).

In "De l'art de persuader," Pascal was already arguing that "the best books are those whose readers believe they could have produced themselves" (p. 427). Reading Pascal, because he expresses himself in a natural style and does not rule out repetitions, it is as though I were finding in myself the truths that he is seeking; I listen to him as if I myself were the seeker.

This is the way Pascal read Montaigne, from whom he drew so much inspiration: "It is not in Montaigne but in myself that I find everything I see there" (568), he asserted, defending his reading method. Pascal does not distance himself from Montaigne but finds himself in him, recognizes and comes to know himself in him. Montaigne was his "writing teacher," as Jean Mesnard was wont to say.

And Proust was to observe: "It is only out of a habit derived from the insincere language of prefaces and dedications that writers talk about 'my reader.' In reality each reader, when he is reading, is uniquely reading himself" (*Finding Time Again,* p. 240). Pascal, after Montaigne, had already conceived of reading as reading oneself in the book of another.

27

The Three Concupiscences

Pascal liked distinctions and classifications. By twos: justice and might, heart and reason. Or, better, by threes: bodies, minds, and charity. Here is another key Pascalian triad, the three desires: "Everything in the world is concupiscence of the flesh or concupiscence of the eyes or pride of life. *Libido sentiendi, libido sciendi, libido dominandi*" (460).

Concupiscence, we must remember, was born with Adam's sin, with the love of creatures substituted for the love of God. It is the opposite of charity.

The starting point for the three forms of concupiscence is found in a quotation from Saint John, in the first letter: "Because nothing the world has to offer—the sensual body, the lustful eye, pride in possessions—could ever come from the Father, but only from the world" (1 John 2:16). Desire in the sense of concupiscence, for Saint Augustine, whom Pascal is following, is not only carnal in nature; it also gives rise to curiosity and to pride or arrogance, the three sources of human corruption "from which all vices and crimes flow," according to Jansen.

The concupiscence of the flesh, or *libido sentiendi,* is easy to understand: it is the temptation of sensuous pleasure, a disorderly desire for voluptuous delight.

Curiosity, or *libido sciendi,* is the excessive desire to know, not the will to engage with the legitimate sciences but to penetrate what is not meant to be known by humankind. Bad science seeks knowledge of divine truths, which are not made for the human mind because they surpass its natural capacities. One must not try to penetrate the secrets of God: *eritis sicut dii scientes bonum et malum:* if you eat the forbidden fruit "you will be like gods, knowing good and evil" (Genesis 3:5).

Finally, pride, *libido dominandi* or the temptation of power, the will to power, is at the root of all concupiscence since the original sin was a sin of pride, an arrogant rebellion against God. We come back to the Pascalian analysis of greatness and might: the pride of the great, like that of the rich, consists in the idea they are self-made through their own might.

The three concupiscences are brought up in connection with the three orders in a fragment of the *Pensées* that Pascal did not retain in one of the labeled sheaves: "*Concupiscence of the flesh, concupiscence of the eyes, pride, etc.* / There are three orders of things: flesh, mind, will. / The carnal are the rich, the kings: their object is the body. / The curious and the learned: their object is the mind. / The wise: their object is justice. . . . / In things of the flesh, concupiscence reigns properly. In things of the mind, curiosity reigns properly. In wisdom, pride reigns properly" (761).

Wisdom does not guarantee humility, then, nor does it exclude pride. The gradation requires additional steps toward faith.

Thus, the three concupiscences define our condition. The remedy for them lies in humility and mortification. Religion allows human beings to "elevate themselves in the inner feeling that remains in them from their past greatness" (240); it allows them to combat the despair with which the concupiscences are associated and to seek a middle ground between wretchedness and greatness, not an Aristotelian "happy medium" but rather a coincidence of two contradictory truths. It is a middle ground in the sense that Christ is a mediator between the divine and the human: Jesus is fully human and fully divine.

> Unhappy is the accursed land that those three rivers of fire set ablaze rather than water! Happy are those who, being on those rivers, not immersed, not carried along, but firmly immobilized on those rivers, not standing but sitting down, in a low and secure seat. (460)

Pascal was one of the happy ones after his "night of fire," an escapee from the three libidos, a returnee from flesh and money, from science and glory. One wonders who it was, at the Banque de France in 1968, who had the strange idea of putting Pascal's portrait on the largest banknote, the "500 francs Pascal" that occasionally turned up in our wallets.

28

The Mystery of Predestination

Grace is far and away the greatest mystery of the Christian religion. In order to justify Port-Royal, Pascal tried to elucidate it with the rigor of a mathematician and the methods of a logician:

> Sinners purified without penitence, just men sanctified without charity, all Christians without the grace of Jesus Christ, God without power over the will of men, predestination without mystery. A redeemer without certainty. (439)

Such is Pascal's list of the errors committed by the Jesuits. He pursued his attack in the *Provincial Letters* after he had developed his own doctrine more fully in his "Writings on Grace," a text he began in 1655, shortly after his definitive conversion.

According to the Jesuits, "sufficient grace" suffices for Christians to be saved, without the requirement that God also give them his "efficacious grace." At Port-Royal, the Jesuits were said to be renewing the Pelagian heresy that Augustine had opposed. Pelagius ascribed too much importance to the freedom of those working toward their salvation and not enough to the grace of God. Every Christian was thought to be able to achieve holiness by their own powers and by exercising their free will; divine grace was thus not indispensable. Against Pelagius, Saint Augustine defended the primacy of salvation through grace. Pelagianism was in his eyes a heresy: if one needs only the forces of one's own nature to carry out God's commandments, then Christ's sacrifice on the cross was useless.

The relation between divine grace and human freedom became a controversial question again when the Calvinists asserted absolute predestination. In reaction the Council of Trent condemned their annihilation of free will but also condemned the notion that one could be saved by one's works alone, without grace. Now, for the Jesuits, at least as Pascal presented them, it was up to humans to obtain salvation or not, by using their free will. Under the influence of humanism and as a way of opposing Protestantism, the Jesuits were breaking with the doctrine of Saint Augustine, confirmed by Saint Thomas, for whom God alone determined who would be saved or not, by granting individuals grace or not.

The conflict between Jesuits and Jansenists was based on the difference between sufficient grace (given by God to everyone) and efficacious grace (given only to the elect). For Pascal and the Jansenists, we achieve salvation only if God grants us grace. Only divine grace can sustain us in faith and make us persevere. Merit and effort do not suffice to obtain grace, which is reserved for the elect. The Jesuits, who attribute to works the prerogative of salvation, appear more human; still, Pascal mocks them in the *Provincial Letters*:

> "But tell me, Father, is this grace given to all men *sufficient*?"
>
> "Yes," he said.
>
> "And yet it is of no effect without efficacious grace?"
>
> "That is true," he said.
>
> "That means," I said, "that all have enough grace, and all do not have enough; that this grace suffices, although it does not suffice; that it is sufficient in name but not sufficient in effect." (*PL* 2, p. 44)

The mystery of grace remains impenetrable. There would be no mystery if all were saved or if all were damned. If some are saved and others damned, that could be attributable to God's justice and mercy. The mystery is that "of two equally guilty [persons]" ("Writings on Grace," *OC* 3:610), or two equally just, God saves the one and not the other without taking their works into account. Saint Augustine ascribes God's discernment "to a just but hidden judgment" ("Writings on Grace," *OC* 3:611), and Pascal reminds us that God chooses his elect "by a hidden and impenetrable judgment" ("Writings on Grace," *OC* 3:682). The mystery is just as great concerning the gift of perseverance: "The reason why, of two just men, one perseveres and the other does not, is an absolutely incomprehensible secret" (Writings on Grace," *OC* 3:671).

Despite Pascal's prodigious dialectics, the Jansenist doctrine of grace remains obscure. The relation between grace and freedom, between predestination and works, seems impenetrable. To deny individual freedom is heretical; to deny the necessity of grace is also heretical. Here again, Pascal gets out of the impasse by presenting the Jansenist doctrine of grace as a coincidence of opposing truths: we are predestined; we are free. Does this not entail renouncing geometry? Pascal concludes

> that God sent Jesus Christ for the salvation solely of those whom
> he had chosen and predestined. . . . It is for their salvation alone
> that Jesus Christ died, and that the others, for whose salvation he
> did not die, have not been delivered from that universal and just
> perdition. ("Writings on Grace," *OC* 3:788)

This thesis, which seems to contest the goodness of God, is indeed one of the five propositions condemned by the pope in the 1653 bull *Cum occasione*. One may think that the thesis presents a more realistic view of our terrestrial world than that of the Jesuits. This world is one in which grace would be simply another name for Fortune—that is, the injustice of life, the inequality of fate among humans.

29

The Mystery of the Holy Thorn

Many fragments in the *Pensées* have to do with miracles. Yet Pascal set them aside in 1658 when he drew up the plan for his apologia for religion. These fragments remind us that the apologia began as a text about miracles, before Pascal decided to introduce it by developing an anthropology, a depiction of the condition of humanity without God.

Here is the problem: since the truth does not reveal itself unveiled, the miracles that attest to it are very useful, but it is difficult if not impossible to distinguish true miracles from false ones precisely because the truth is hidden, which is why miracles can be abused.

Here is by no means the land of truth. Truth wanders unknown among men. God has covered it with a veil that leaves it unrecognizable to those who do not hear its voice. The place is open to blasphemy. . . . The truth that the doctrine must be supported by miracles is abused in order to blaspheme the doctrine. And if miracles

happen, it is said that miracles do not suffice without the doctrine,
and this is another truth misused to blaspheme miracles. (425)

If Pascal was so interested in miracles, it is because his project
for the apologia originated in a miracle that affected him very
closely. Marguerite Périer, his niece and goddaughter, age ten at the
time, a boarding school student at Port-Royal in Paris, suffered
from an illness that the doctors could not cure. First, "some drops"
flowed out of one of her eyes, then the infection spread, emitting a
strong odor through the child's mouth and nose. According to the
account by her mother, Gilberte, of an event that was said to have
taken place on March 24, 1656:

> It was at that time that it pleased God to cure my daughter of a
> lacrimal fistula that had advanced so much in three and a half years
> that pus was coming out of not only her eye but inside her nose
> and through her mouth. And the fistula was so bad that the best
> surgeons in Paris deemed it incurable. Nevertheless, she was cured
> in an instant, by the application of a Holy Thorn; and this miracle
> was so authentic that it was widely acknowledged, having been at-
> tested by very great doctors and by the most gifted surgeons of
> France, and having been authorized by a solemn judgment of the
> Church. (*OC* 1:583)

The miracle was timely, for it occurred at the very moment
Port-Royal was being attacked by the ecclesiastical authorities.
Approved after an investigation by the archbishop of Paris in October 1656, it had immense repercussions. Pascal, who was
working on the *Provincial Letters* at the time, drew from it an argument in defense of Port-Royal:

Here is a sacred relic, here is a thorn from the crown of the Savior of the world, . . . that makes miracles by the very power of the blood that was shed for us. Here is this house that God himself chose so that his power could shine forth there." (434)

There was no doubt, then, that the truth was on the side of the Jansenists:

This house is God's, for he produced strange miracles there. The others [say]: That house is not God's, for those in it do not believe that the five propositions are in Jansen. Which is the clearer? (435)

Their adversaries, in contrast, manifested bad faith: "Unjust persecutors of those whom God visibly protects" (438).

On one side, the miracle is interpreted as a sign favorable to Port-Royal; on the other, as a sham. Pascal's project thus made its debut as a reflection on miracles in order to convince the atheists. According to Gilberte: "And that was the occasion that gave birth in him to the extreme desire he had to work to refute the principal and strongest reasonings of the atheists. He had studied them with great care and he had put his whole mind to seeking ways to convince them" (OC 1:584).

Pascal sought to define miracles, their conditions, their proofs; he accumulated fragments on the topic until June 1658, when he produced a classification that downgraded them and defined the apologetic project quite differently:

Men have contempt for religion, they have hatred for it, and fear that it might be true. To cure this one has to begin by showing that religion is not at all contrary to reason. Venerable, eliciting respect. Next make it appealing, make good men wish that it were true, and then show that it is true. / Venerable, because it has known humanity well. Appealing, because it promises the true good. (46)

30

The Middle Ground

In a world always and everywhere divided between pros and cons, Pascal set out to find the position that would supersede contradictions, that would be equidistant from the two extremes, or that would rise above them:

> Extreme intelligence is accused of madness; so is its extreme lack. Nothing but mediocrity is good: it is the plurality that has established this, and that constantly chastises anyone who deviates from it in any direction whatsoever. I shall not belabor the point. I fully accept being located there, and I refuse to be at the low end, not because it is low but because it is an endpoint, for I would likewise refuse to be placed at the top. Leaving the middle is to leave humanity. (452)

Mediocrity, here, does not have a derogatory meaning. On the contrary, situated between two extremes it sins neither by excess nor by lack, and it corresponds to the ideal of the aurea mediocritas, Horatio's "precious moderation." A philosophy of the middle ground, it advocates temperance. Pascal's pseudonym in the *Pensées* is Salomon de Tultie, linking the wisdom of Solomon and madness, *sultitia* in Latin: neither sage nor madman, or rather both at once.

Pascal positions himself on the side of the plurality, or the majority, in his defense of mediocrity. Thanks to a gradation, the wise person joins in the opinion of the people against the half-clever persons who want to stand out from the crowd.

When someone like Montaigne claims the middle—neither the bottom nor the top end, neither the most honorable place nor the least honorable—this corresponds to his acceptance of the human condition, for greatness consists in staying in the middle; but this attitude is surprising on Pascal's part: What is a middle between two infinities?

> For, finally, what is man in nature? Nothing with respect to the infinite, everything with respect to nothingness, a middle between nothing and everything, infinitely remote from grasping the extremities. (230)

The place in the middle would thus offer man no comfort:

> There are [only] three sorts of persons: those who serve God, having found him; those who spend their time seeking him, not having found him; those who live without seeking him and without having found him. The first are reasonable and happy; the last are mad and unhappy. Those in the middle are unhappy and reasonable. (192)

A geometrician likes combinatorics: he reasons by listing all possible logical positions. Having set aside the other combinations,

Pascal addresses those people who are reasonable and unhappy, those who seek without having yet found. We can recognize ourselves in those seekers, whatever the goal of our search may be—for God or the meaning of life.

The middle is not, for Pascal, a compromise but the surpassing of two simplistic positions—another instance of dialectical gradation. It is harder, not easier, to conquer than the two extremes.

> And it usually happens that, unable to conceive of the relation between two opposite truths and believing that the acknowledgment of the one encompasses the exclusion of the other, they commit to the one and exclude the other, while thinking that we do the opposite. Now, this exclusion is the cause of their heresy, and their unawareness that we cling to the other causes their objections. (614)

Pascal often comes back to the middle as a coincidence of opposites. Thus, the hidden God occupies the middle, between being veiled and uncovered: "If God revealed himself continuously to man, there would be no merit in believing him; and if he never revealed himself, there would be little faith," Pascal wrote to Mlle de Roannez in October 1656, playing the role of spiritual director and setting forth for her his conception of the hidden God (*OC* 3:1035).

But the equilibrium remains fragile:

> Knowledge of God without that of one's own wretchedness produces pride. / Knowledge of one's own wretchedness without knowledge of God produces despair. / Knowledge of Jesus Christ produces the middle ground because we find there both God and our own wretchedness. (225)

Between pride and despair, neither one nor the other or both at once: such, according to Pascal, is the position of the man of faith: reasonably unhappy.

The procedure is the same as in the conversation with M. de Sacy when Pascal is navigating between Epictetus and Montaigne. But isn't all that a bit too stiff and formal?

Let us end with some more frivolous examples: "Two Infinities. Middle. / When one reads too fast or too slowly one understands nothing" (601).

Or this one: "Too much and too little wine. Don't give him any, he can't find the truth. Give him too much, the same" (72).

Between slowness and speed, drunkenness and sobriety, how to keep the measure, how to find the middle ground, the fixed point? This is as hard to do in reading as in all quests, in the search for God as in the search for truth or the meaning of life.

31

Double Thoughts

A man is tossed by a storm onto an unknown island, whose inhabitants were struggling to find their king, who had been lost; and,
since he bore a great resemblance in face and body to that king,
the man was taken for him and recognized as such by all the
people. At first he did not know what to do; but he finally resolved
to go along with his good fortune. He received all the gestures
of respect that were offered him, and he let himself be treated
as king.

—OC 4:1029

Pascal was a geometrician and a
strict logician, but he was not lacking in real talent as a storyteller.
He denounced imagination as a "mistress of error and falsehood,"
but he liked fables and did not hesitate to invent some to convince
his interlocutors. One of his most seductive parables opens the
first of the three "Discourses on the Condition of the Great." In a
conversation reported by his friend Pierre Nicole, Pascal was

giving a lesson to the duc de Chevreuse, the oldest son of the duc de Luynes. He wanted the young man, destined to be among the greats, not to confuse the social role with the self, the private person. Montaigne said: "We must play our part duly, but as the part of a borrowed character. Of the mask and appearance we must not make a real essence, nor of what is foreign what is our very own" (*Essays,* bk. 3, chap. 10, p. 941). Pascal enriches this old commonplace in his story of a shipwreck victim taken to be their king by a remote people. This is an opportunity to meditate on the condition of the great and on the human condition in general. This man became king by chance, following a mistake on the part of the inhabitants of the island who had lost their sovereign. The anecdote illustrates the contingency of our condition: nothing justifies our privileges, our rank, whatever it may be, not even our birth and our existence, which are in no sense necessary. This is why Pascal advises the young man not to entertain any illusions about the condition that will be his in the world but to follow the example of the "acting" king in his unknown island:

> As he could not forget his natural condition, he reflected, while he was receiving this respect, that he was not the king the people were seeking, and that this kingdom did not belong to him. Thus he had double thoughts, one through which he acted as a king, another through which he recognized his real state, and that it was only chance that had put him in the place he was occupying; he hid that latter thought, and revealed the other. It was through the first that he dealt with the people, and through the second that he dealt with himself. (*OC* 4:1029)

It is a question of playing our role well before others but not letting our inner selves be duped by it. These "double thoughts" that Pascal describes oppose one's social condition—power, wealth, prestige—to one's true being. He is addressing an aristocrat, but the lesson would be the same in a democracy. In the sheaf of the *Pensées* labeled "Vanity," Pascal notes that "the Swiss are offended if they are called gentlemen, and they prove their common birth so as to be judged worthy of the highest tasks" (83), thereby stressing the arbitrariness of political systems: here gentlemen hold responsibilities, there the commoners do so, in both cases by convention.

And it is not just his condition of greatness that Pascal asks the young nobleman to keep at a distance but indeed the human condition, which is equally unjustified:

> Don't imagine that you possess the riches of which you find yourself the master by some lesser chance than that by which that man found himself king. You have no right to them on your own, or by your nature, any more than he did: and not only do you find yourself the son of a duke, but you find yourself existing in the world only as a result of an infinite number of chance events. Your birth depends on a marriage, or rather on all the marriages from which you descend. But those marriages: what do they depend on? On a coincidental visit, on a random remark, on a thousand unforeseen occasions. (*OC* 4:1030)

Social life rests on arbitrary conventions, not on a natural order: there is no more telling image of that state of affairs than the shipwreck victim who became a king. Now it happens that all humans are shipwreck victims. Any arrogance or insolence on their part, particularly among the "great," is thus proof of their lying about themselves, their "bad faith," to use the language of Jean-Paul Sartre.

32

"What Is the Self?"

"The self is hateful. You, Mitton, keep it under cover, but you don't remove it. Thus you are still hateful" (494.) Pascal is addressing Damien Mitton, his libertine friend, a theoretician of the honnête homme. *Honnêteté* dissimulates the self, self-love, but does not annihilate it. Pascal attacks his friend: you are hateful, despite your altruism (494). The honnête homme is a hypocrite: thanks to his human civility, his self is not the "center of everything," but only Christian piety can convert self-love into charity.

But the self is not always identified with self-love in the *Pensées:*

> I sense that I might never have been, for my self consists in my thought. Thus the I who thinks would never have existed, had my mother been killed before I had been brought to life. So I am not a necessary being. (167)

The use of the word *moi,* translated here as "self," as a substantive in French, is recent. We find it in Descartes, and this fragment from the *Pensées* recalls Descartes's second "Meditation": "For it could be that were I totally to cease from thinking, I should totally cease to exist" (*Meditations*, p. 37). Pascal, for his part, insists on the contingency of the self. The self lacks necessity, lacks substance, and natural philosophy is incapable of justifying its existence.

Another paradoxical fragment from the *Pensées* actually has "What Is the Self?" as its title:

> Given a man standing at a window to see the passers-by: if I pass by, can I say that he was standing there in order to see me? No, for he is not thinking about me in particular. But consider the man who loves someone because of her beauty: does he love her? No, for smallpox, which will kill beauty without killing the person, will make him no longer love her. (567)

It has been noted that Pascal's highly beloved sister Jacqueline had facial scars after contracting smallpox at the age of thirteen. But readers of Pascal have most often been reminded of a page in Descartes's *Meditations* about men who are passing by in the street. How can we know, Descartes asks, whether the form that is passing under a hat is a man or an automaton? Pascal uses the scene differently. He does not ask whether, for the observer, the passersby are really men but whether the man at his window is expecting him, *himself*.

The self here is not self-love but what distinguishes an individual, what makes someone a person. In the framework of natural philosophy, the self is an undeniable reality whose immediate presence we can sense, but this reality is incomprehensible. Every individual is a person, but that person is indefinable.

We must be careful not to get this wrong. Pascal does not maintain that there is no self but that it is impossible to determine the essence of any self. The self is neither a substance nor an accident. The love one has for someone is inseparable from that person's beauty, and if the beauty disappears, Pascal asserts, the love is destroyed. What does it mean to love if one loves for beauty and if beauty is an accident? It means that the object of that love was not the being, the self, of the other. The self—that mysterious unity of the soul of which we nevertheless have immediate certainty—is inaccessible.

This question besets Pascal:

> And if someone loves me for my judgment, for my memory, does he love me myself? No, for I can lose those qualities without losing myself. Where is this self, then, if it is neither in the body nor in the soul? And can one love the body or the soul apart from its qualities, which are not at all what makes the self, since they are perishable? For would one love the substance of a person's soul abstractly, and no matter what qualities it might have? That cannot be, and it would be unjust. So we never love anyone, but only love qualities. (567)

It is no longer a question of the beauty of the body but of the faculties, judgment, and memory, intellectual realities emanating from the soul:

> I can readily conceive of a man without hands, feet or head, since it is only experience that teaches us that the head is more necessary than the feet. But I cannot conceive of a man without thought. It would be a stone, or a beast. (143)

Judgment and memory are attributes of thought. But the self does not disappear in the person who loses them, in an insane person or someone with amnesia. We run up against an aporia, and the self remains a mystery: "Not knowing by ourselves who we are, we can only learn this from God" (182).

One never encounters only qualities. Why then should we not pay our respects to persons of high status? "For the self to be constituted as an authentic being," as Jean Mesnard put it, "grace must link it with the only necessary being, which is God" (*Les Pensées de Pascal,* p. 305).

33

Village Queens and False Windows

Pascal mistrusts rhetoric and its artificial flourishes: "'Put out the flame of sedition': too lush. / 'The anxiety (*inquiétude*) of his genius': two bold words too many" (529). He speaks out against false beauties, against an overabundance, an excess of expressiveness. *Inquiétude* is a very strong word: in its literal sense, it indicates the impossibility of remaining at rest, a state of perpetual agitation. "All the false beauties that we condemn in Cicero have admirers, and in great numbers" (610).

As his sister Gilberte said, no "fine thoughts" or "false brilliance" were in him, "never fancy words, and few metaphorical expressions, nothing obscure or crude, nothing overbearing, nothing left out, nothing superfluous" (*OC* 1:617). Pascal hated fancy words. The last sentence of "De l'art de persuader" puts it bluntly: "I hate those pompous words" (p. 145).

One fragment of the *Pensées* is titled "Poetic Beauty," and it is a warning:

We do not know what the natural model that we are supposed to imitate is, and for want of that knowledge certain bizarre terms have been invented: "golden age," "wonder of our time," "fatal," etc. And this jargon is called poetic beauty. (486)

Pascal does not often broach the topic of women. However, he turns to the traditional image of feminine beauty to express his mistrust of poetry as ornaments and jewels:

But the man who will imagine a woman on that model, which consists in saying petty things with big words, will see a pretty girl encumbered with mirrors and chains, and he will laugh at her, because one knows better what makes for attractive women than for attractive verses. But those who lack that knowledge would admire her in that outfit and there are many villages where she would be taken for the queen. And that is why we call sonnets built on that model village queens. (486)

Pascal defends classic decorum, where there is proportionality between words and things, against baroque mannerisms, where that proportionality is lacking; he mistrusts the "village queens" who delude poetry lovers. This attitude irritated Voltaire and led Sainte-Beuve to express a reservation: "However great Pascal's genius may be, there are countless true and great things that, perhaps because of his era or especially because of his nature, . . . he does not go into and has no intention of going into. Let us list a few: he has no feel for poetry, he rejects it; and poetry is a whole essential part of man, even of a religious man" (*Port-Royal*, pp. 38–39).

He has an explicit antipathy to antitheses:

Those who make antitheses by forcing the words are acting like those who make false windows for symmetry. / Their rule is not to speak aptly but to make apt figures of speech. (466)

And yet the taste for antitheses is manifest in his own writing, in conformity with the dialectical method and the shift "from for to against" (124):

If he exalts himself, I humble him.

If he humbles himself, I exalt him.

And I continue to contradict him

Until he comprehends

That he is an incomprehensible monster. (163)

Given its formal layout, some have characterized this fragment as a poem.

Still another paradox: rhetorical delicacy is more violent in its effects than brusque eloquence. This is a way to read one expeditious fragment: "Eloquence that persuades by gentleness not by empire, as a tyrant not a king" (485). Gentleness is associated with tyranny, always defined as a transgression of the boundary between orders, whereas empire, a legitimate force, is associated with the king. This is because the rhetoric of gentleness is addressed not to the understanding but to the will, to desire, which treats what pleases it as just; it derives from an art of causing pleasure rather than from an art of convincing. The gentle manner is imposing: not allowing the interlocutors to figure things out for themselves, it tyrannizes them.

This is why Pascal's manner, in the *Provincial Letters* and the *Pensées,* is in no way gentle; it is characterized by great vehemence. He is rough on his libertine friends, on whom he does not hesitate to heap invective so that they will react: "You are still hateful," he scolds Mitton (494).

Yes, but gentleness also characterizes God's action: "God's way, which is to address all things with gentleness, is to instill religion in the mind with reasons and in the heart with grace" (203).

A new instance of the coincidence of opposites.

34

"*Working for What Is Uncertain*"

"The people have very healthy opinions. For example: / . . . Working for what is uncertain, going to sea, crossing on a plank" (134). Here is another instance of the "cause of effects": semiclever people are skeptical of enterprises whose results appear to be matters of chance, whereas common people agree to "work for what is uncertain." Yet the semiclever are wrong, while the people are right, and their opinion is legitimate: they have the intuition of the "rule for the division of stakes," a name that Pascal gave to the future calculus of probabilities.

Is it worthwhile to "work for what is uncertain"? "Going to sea" is for Pascal the model of a risky enterprise. And yet people do this (perhaps they don't have a choice). As for "crossing on a plank," this is reminiscent of the classic example of the power of the imagination, taken up again by Montaigne and then by Pascal in the long fragment "Imagination" of the *Pensées:*

> [Imagine] the greatest philosopher in the world on a plank wider
> than is necessary. If there is a precipice underneath, even though
> his reason convinces him of his safety, his imagination will prevail.
> Some would be unable to subscribe to the thought without
> growing pale and perspiring. (78)

A man of the people will be more willing than a philosopher to
walk along a plank stretched over a void. This plank might be the
one that must be crossed to board a boat and "go to sea."

Pascal, the pioneer analyst of probabilities, demonstrates what
he labels the "rule of probability" in his 1654 "Treatise on the Arithmetic Triangle." The third section is titled "Use of the Arithmetic
Triangle to Determine the Divisions That Must Be Established between Two Gamblers Who Are Playing a Number of Games." This
rule states that "the proportional relation between the uncertainty of winning and the certainty about what one is wagering is
determined by the odds of winning or losing" (680); in other
words, the mathematical expectation is the winner's reward mul-
tiplied by the probability of winning, and it makes it possible to
determine rationally the most advantageous choice to make in
a situation of uncertainty. The notion comes from games of
chance, a diversion enjoyed by Pascal's libertine friends Méré
and Mitton: Pascal seeks to determine how to distribute the
stakes when a contest is interrupted before all the games have
been played.

And Pascal applies this rule of probability to life:

> One must live differently in the world, depending on these diverse
> suppositions: / Whether one could be there always. / Whether it is

certain that one will not be there for long, and whether it is uncertain that one can be there for an hour. / This last supposition is
ours. (187)

He thinks that his libertine honnête homme will be amenable to
rational arguments like these. He accumulates them in the *Pensées*
in the sheaf "Beginning," a transition between the anthropological
and theological parts of his argument.

> If one should do nothing except in certainty, one should do nothing
> for religion, for it is uncertain. But how many things do we do in
> uncertainty: sea voyages, battles! I say, then, that we should do
> nothing at all, for nothing is certain, and there is more certainty
> in religion than there is certainty that we shall see the light of day
> tomorrow. (480)

A nonbeliever or a semiclever individual speaks first. It is reasonable, he says, to do nothing for religion, which is uncertain. Pascal
objects, in response, that people take great risks in conducting business, such as going to sea or making war. Why should they behave
differently where religion is concerned? Pascal demands consis-
tency on his interlocutor's part, for "it is not certain that everything is uncertain" (453).

Between today and tomorrow, a cosmic accident might prevent
us from seeing daylight. One can assert with certainty that it is possible that the world will end tomorrow, but one cannot assert with
certainty that it is possible that God does not exist:

> For it is not certain that we shall see tomorrow, but it is certainly
> possible that we shall not see it. One cannot say the same of reli-
> gion. It is not certain that it will endure. But who would dare to

> say that it is certainly possible it will not? Now, when we work for
> tomorrow and for the uncertain we act with reason. / For one must
> work for the uncertain, according to the rule of probability, which
> has been demonstrated. / St. Augustine saw that we work for the
> uncertain: at sea, in battle, etc., but he did not see the rule of prob-
> ability, which demonstrated that we must. (480)

Saint Augustine charged with vanity those who devoted their
time and effort to going to sea or to war for unpredictable results,
but he did not see the cause of effects—that is, the rule of the probability and a mathematically elevated hope. Even Saint Augustine
could behave, like Montaigne, as a semiclever individual—on this
point at least. Flush with praise for his mathematical invention,
Pascal still had a way to go in the matter of humility.

35

"Infinite Nothingness"

In the film *My Night at Maud's,* the characters expound freely on Pascal's wager. Often, it is the only thing we recall from the *Pensées.* But what is it about? Is it really the essence?

We are incapable of knowing God, either what he is or if he is. "Natural insights" are of no use to us, and Christians cannot account logically for their faith. Is Pascal running up against an impasse in his apologia for religion? No, for it is here that he resorts to the model of games, of "parties," as he says in order to push his libertine to make a decision:

> So let us examine this point and say: God is, or he is not. But to which side shall we lean? Reason can determine nothing here. An infinite chaos separates us. A game is being played, at one extreme of this infinite distance, where it will land heads or tails: what will you wager? Reason does not allow you to pick one or the other; rationally you cannot defend either of the two. (680)

Let's make no mistake here: the purpose of the wager is not to demonstrate the existence of God. That existence is uncertain, and the libertine, who behaves like a semiclever individual, responds that, in uncertainty,

> "the best thing is not to bet." The apologist counters: "Yes, but it's imperative to bet. It isn't voluntary: you're committed. So which will you pick? Let's see. Since you have to choose, let's see which is least in your interest. You have two things to lose, the true and the good, and two things to commit, your reason and your will, your knowledge and your beatitude; and your nature has two things to flee, error and wretchedness. Since you necessarily have to choose, your reason isn't more wounded one way or the other. Here is one point disposed of. But your beatitude? Let's weigh the gain and the loss in making the choice that God exists. Let's assess these two cases: if you win, you win everything; if you lose, you lose nothing. Bet, then, that he exists, without hesitation!" (680)

If one wins because God exists, one wins everything; if one loses because God does not exist, one loses nothing since nothingness cannot make the player pay for one's mistake.

Pascal goes into mathematical detail: If there were only two lives to win, the wager would be equitable, and why not place the bet? If there were three to win, the bet would become advantageous, and it would be imprudent not to play. But there is an infinity of life to win: it is thus unreasonable not to bet. And even if there were not one chance in two that God exists but one out of infinity, since there would be an infinity of life to win, the bet would still be balanced and worthwhile:

In every case where there is infinity and where there is not an infinity of chances to lose against the chance of winning, there is nothing to weigh, one must give everything. (680)

Still, the libertine hasn't made up his mind: "I confess, I admit it, but still. . . . Isn't there another way to see what underlies the game?" (680).

We are at a turning point. The libertine is convinced of the rational necessity of betting, but he does not place his bet:

My hands are tied and I am mute. I am being forced to bet, and I am not at liberty, I cannot get away. And I am made in such a way that I cannot believe. (680)

To which the apologist replies:

That is true. But learn at least that your inability to believe, since reason impels you to do so and since even so you cannot do it, [comes] from your passions. Work then, not to convince yourself by adding proofs of God, but by diminishing your passions. (680)

The argument of the wager shows only that the libertine, who fancies himself rational, is not behaving rationally when he refuses to believe. Thus, he must be made aware of the role of the passions, of self-love, in his resistance. The challenge is no longer to find a convincing argument but to make the libertine open to it.

In the face of his interlocutor's persistent doubt, Pascal changes tactics and recommends that he behave like those who believe: "Follow the way they took at the start: it is by acting just as though they believed, taking the holy water, having masses said, etc. That will even make you believe naturally and will make you more beast-like." "But that is exactly what I fear." "And why? What do you have to lose?" (680).

To make oneself beast-like is not to become stupid but to behave like an animal—that is, like a "machine" (39). Pascal, after Descartes, conceives of the body as an automaton. To adopt the posture of belief (41) is to allow custom to serve as the pathway to faith: the belief produced by habit is "easier." Thus, it behooves us, before truly believing, to follow the habitual behaviors of believers, for "we are as much automaton as mind" (661). There is no longer anything mathematical about the argument.

The final argument: making the bet brings a supplementary benefit, an immediate reward in this life itself:

> Now, what harm will befall you if you commit to this cause? You will be faithful, honest, humble, grateful, beneficent, a true and sincere friend. . . . I tell you that you will profit from it in this life. (680)

In short, by betting you win in any case—if not in an afterlife, then at least here below. It would thus be truly idiotic not to do it.

36

Private Vice, Public Good

Pascal, convinced of original sin, was a pessimist, but his pessimism paradoxically led him, like some other seventeenth-century moralists, to prefigure a certain modern optimism. In his way, he set the stage for Adam Smith and liberalism, as did Bernard Mandeville with his *Fable of the Bees* (1714), a primer of capitalism: egoistic self-love drives us to seek wealth and power; by freeing desires, vice contributes to social wealth and order; from individual vice, collective prosperity involuntarily arises. "Private vices produce public good," according to the maxim.

A related idea appears in the margins of the *Pensées:* from individual disorder comes collective order; in the competition among desires deriving from the original sin, an equilibrium is established. Saint Augustine already emphasized in *Concerning the City of God* that "even *what is perverted must of necessity be in, or derived from, or associated with—that is, in a sense, at peace with—some part of the order among which it has its being or of which it consists. Otherwise it would not exist at all*" (bk. 19, chap. 12, p. 869). War, he said, "is waged by or within persons who are in some sense natural beings—for they could have no kind of existence without some kind of peace as the condition of their being" (bk. 19, chap. 12, p. 871).

In the "Wretchedness" sheaf of the *Pensées,* Pascal declared: "They have found no other way to satisfy their concupiscence without doing harm to others" (108). Political systems enable men whose self-love and concupiscence would lead them to subjugate and destroy each other to live together. The social order regulates desires, and each person is satisfied to leave the others free to satisfy themselves: "Greatness of man even in concupiscence, for having been able to draw from it an admirable set of rules and having turned it into a picture of charity" (150).

But can the collective order drawn from individual concupiscences really present "a picture of charity"? The reasoning is once again more paradoxical or dialectical: the wretchedness of human beings proves their greatness; concupiscence, or self-love, engenders an admirable society, a "picture of charity," that is, a figure of the love of God.

The *libido dominandi,* the order of the flesh, produces the kings, the rich men, the captains who produce order in civil society. Thus, the aggregation of individual egoisms does not lead to the law of the jungle and anarchy but rather to a genuine order.

However, this picture of order is necessarily false: the figure of charity is necessarily deceptive. The order of a society of concupiscence owes nothing to charity but is only its image, its simulacrum. Thus, in the sheaf "Falsity of the Other Religions": "All men naturally hate one another. Some have been able to use concupiscence to make it serve the public good. But this is only a feint and a false image of charity. For at bottom it is only hatred" (243).

For concupiscence, a ferment of disorder, to be satisfied, there needs to be a certain order governing society. A relative, superficial, and precarious peace has to reign in order for the cravings to exert themselves, as in the zones set apart by the Onorata Società or any other Mafia-style organization. But the order of such a civil society is based on hatred, not on charity. There is little difference between the society that complies with the ideal of the honnête homme and one in which, in order to be satisfied, each person's self-love makes accommodations with the self-love of others.

> People have established and drawn from concupiscence admirable rules for policies, morals, and justice. / But at bottom that ugly underpinning of man, this FIGMENTUM MALUM, is only concealed. It is not removed. (244)

We are not quite at the level of the *Fable of the Bees* and the justification of capitalism. Pascal does not claim that vices are profitable, but he does say that self-love is capable of limiting itself and of regulating concupiscence in such a way that it no longer bothers others excessively and that the others moderate their own egoism in return: self-love itself neutralizes the tyranny of the self over the others. This is what Freud will call repression.

37

"*You Would Not Be Seeking Me if
You Had Not Found Me*"

"One of the most mistreated sentences in French literature is certainly Pascal's 'You would not be seeking me, if you had not found me,'" Julien Green notes in his *Journal*. "It is nevertheless uncomplicated, at least on the surface" (4:1146).

This sentence appears in "The Mystery of Jesus," a meditation in the *Pensées* drafted in early 1655, perhaps during Pascal's stay at Port-Royal-des-Champs after the revelation of the "night of fire." That title, "The Mystery of Jesus," is not Pascal's, but it befits his undertaking: Pascal is seeking the spiritual meaning of the events of Jesus's life, principally following the Gospel according to Saint Matthew.

Jesus suffers in his Passion the torments inflicted on him by men. But in his agony he suffers the torments he inflicts on himself. . . .

It is torture from a non-human but all-powerful hand. And one
must be all-powerful to bear it. . . . / He suffers that pain and that
abandonment in the horror of the night. / I believe that Jesus never
complained except this once. But this time he complains as if he
could no longer bear his excessive suffering: "I am deeply grieved,
even unto death." / Jesus will be in agony until the world's end. One
must not sleep during that time. (749)

It is after this meditation that we come upon these words of en-
couragement: "Take comfort, you would not be seeking me if you
had not found me" (751).

Once again, the formulation is paradoxical or even circular, for
it tries to grasp the nature of grace, and grace is a mystery. Pascal
was trying to get beyond the contradiction between the Calvinists
and the Molinists in his "Writings on Grace," trying to reconcile
predestination and free will, but it is not clear that he succeeded in
doing anything but beg the question.

He took his inspiration here from Saint Bernard of Clairvaux:
"Nemo quaerere te valet, nisi qui prius invenerit" (No one can seek
you who has not already found you; "Treatise on the Love of God,"
chap. 7, p. 41).

Since every quest is the effect of grace, to seek God is to be
sought by him. The quest is an act of God as well as a human act.
This is what makes Pascal write in his "Text on the Conversion of
the Sinner" about the contradictions of the soul traversed by grace
and *a contrario:* God "cannot be taken away from those who reject
him since to possess him is to desire him and to refuse him is to lose
him" (*OC* 4:42–43).

He has just mentioned "the habit of piety"—that is, the "machine," the respect for rituals that lead to a first belief, then "reason helped by the light of grace," the second stage on the pathway to faith. We recognize its three moments: machine, reason, and grace.

As the eminent Pascal scholar Dominique Descotes puts it, "every quest on man's part presupposes that he has already been the object of an appeal on God's part, and that in a certain way he has already found what he is looking for" (*Pascal, auteur spirituel,* p. 437).

It is God who seeks human beings to induce them to be sought by him. God provokes a first rudimentary faith, then, in a second stage, he seeks the one who seeks him:

> There are two ways in which man seeks God; two ways in which God seeks man. . . . For the way in which God seeks man when he gives man the feeble beginnings of faith in order to cause man to cry out to him, in view of his disarray, *Lord, seek your servant,* is very different from the way God seeks man when he answers that prayer, and seeks him in order to be found. For he who said: *seek your servant,* had undoubtedly already been sought and found. But because the man, who had the spirit of prophecy, knew that there was another way in which God could seek him, he used the first way to obtain the second. (*OC* 3:656–657)

Thus, the thought admired by Julien Green had already appeared in that letter, among the "Writings on Grace": any persons who asked God to seek them had unquestionably already been sought and found.

The paradox or the circularity of this thought finds itself, if not resolved, then at least clarified by the description of the two successive quests of humans by God and of God by humans:

> The way we seek God feebly, when he gives us the first wish to take leave of our commitments, is quite different from the way we seek him when, after he has broken off the ties, we head toward him running along the path of his precepts. (*OC* 3:656–657)

But the most important element is the opening: "Take comfort." Pascal will say again, in the *Pensées:* "You would not seek me if you did not already possess me. / Do not worry, then" (756).

Be consoled, don't worry: God addresses human beings, encourages them.

I often repeated this sentence to students who were beginning their research under my direction: "You wouldn't be looking if you hadn't already found." The philosopher Hans-Georg Gadamer defined the hermeneutic circle this way, as a circle, not at all vicious, that grounds the act of understanding (all understanding anticipates the meaning of the whole). It is the principle of all research that Pascal had perfectly formulated; Proust spoke, in this regard, of "Pascal's sublime word."

38

"The Hidden God"

Charlotte de Roannez, the sister of Pascal's friend the duke of Roannez, visited Port-Royal in Paris in August 1656, amid the heated controversy surrounding the *Provincial Letters;* she immediately expressed the desire to live there in retreat as a nun. Her brother took her into the Poitou region so she could put her vocation to the test. An abundant correspondence with Pascal followed, between September 1656 and February 1657. He played the role of spiritual director: without imposing himself, he accompanied her in her conversion. We can see in the letters the emergence of the theme of the hidden God, which will be at the heart of his doctrine in the *Pensées:*

> If God revealed himself continually to men, there would be no merit in believing him; and if he never revealed himself, there would be little faith. But he usually conceals himself, and reveals himself rarely to those whom he wants to enlist in his service. This strange secrecy into which God has withdrawn, impenetrable by

human sight, is a great lesson for our retreat into solitude far from the sight of men. (*OC* 3:1035; ca. October 29, 1656)

Neither always hidden nor always visible, God conceals himself most of the time, but he does reveal himself occasionally. Attention on the part of humankind is all the more necessary in that God is even more hidden when he shows himself:

> He has remained hidden under the veil of nature, which hid him from us until the Incarnation; and when it became necessary for him to appear, he hid himself all the more by covering himself with humanity. He was much more recognizable when he was invisible, and not when he made himself visible. (*OC* 3:1035; ca. October 29, 1656)

Christ, God become human, is also a hidden God, a God even more hidden.

> I believe that Isaiah saw him in that state, when he said in a spirit of prophecy: *Truly you are a hidden God.* There is the last secrecy in which he can be. . . . All things conceal some mystery; all things are veils that conceal God. Christians have to recognize him in everything. (*OC* 3:1036–1037; ca. October 29, 1656)

Hidden "under the veil of nature," hidden under the humanity of the Incarnation, God is also hidden, as Pascal goes on to specify, under the forms of bread and wine in the Eucharist and under the letter of Scripture.

This is why, in the *Pensées,* where the motif of the *Deus absconditus* in the Book of Isaiah (45:15) is recurrent (752), Pascal mocks the theologians who claim that the action of Providence in the world is visible to humans. Scripture, he objects, says, on the contrary, that God is a hidden God; and that, ever since the corruption of nature, he has left men in a blindness from which they can only escape through Jesus Christ, apart from whom all communication with God is withdrawn. . . . This is what Scripture points out to us, when it says in so many places that those who seek God find him. It is not of this light that Scripture is speaking, as in full daylight at noon. It is not saying that those who look for daylight at noon or for water in the sea will find what they are looking for. And so, necessarily, the evidence of God cannot be such as is found in nature. Scripture also tells us, elsewhere: *vere tu es Deus absconditus* [verily, you are a hidden God]. (644)

Pascal intends to show that

hiding himself was God's will. / God being thus hidden, any religion that does not say this is not a true religion, and any religion that does not explain it is not instructive. Ours does all this. (275)

By a dialectical reversal, obscurity is not an argument against the Christian religion, but on the contrary, is in favor of it. The proof that it is the true religion hinges on the very fact that it recognizes that God is hidden, that the truths of religion are immersed in chiaroscuro. Thus, humility and attentiveness are recommended to believers and atheists alike, not assurance and satisfaction. For God hides himself from those who are blinded by self-love but reveals himself to purified hearts:

Instead of complaining that God is hidden, you will thank him for having revealed himself so much, and you will thank him for having not revealed himself to the arrogant wise men who are unworthy of knowing such a holy god. / Two sorts of people know, those whose hearts have been humbled and who embrace lowliness, whatever degree of intelligence they have, high or low, or those who have enough intelligence to see the truth, whatever resistance to it they may harbor. (13)

Here we find another gradation. God shows himself to simple souls and to perspicacious minds but not to the prideful who fall between the two: "It is right that a God so pure should reveal himself only to those whose hearts are purified" (646).

39

Geometrical Mind, Intuitive Mind

A famous pairing that Pascal also instigated and that has passed into common parlance, cited indiscriminately on the radio as well as elsewhere and often "abused," as Julien Green said about another fragment of the *Pensées,* is that of the geometrical mind and the intuitive mind. It is associated a little too readily with the distinction between scientific and literary types, between the "two cultures" set in exaggerated opposition and deemed irreconcilable by C. P. Snow in an unfortunate 1959 lecture in Cambridge. Pascal's analysis is more subtle, actually distinguishing three mindsets: geometry, intuition, and finesse—three attitudes characterized by three ways of reasoning on the basis of principles.

For the geometrical mind,

> the principles are palpable, but remote from common usage, so that one has difficulty turning one's head in that direction, for want of habit. But if one simply turns in that direction, one sees the principles plainly. (670)

Mathematical principles are not available to the senses; they disrupt habits and are "unaccustomed" and counterintuitive, as we would now call them. In Pascal's day, it was the infinite universe opposed to the closed world, or the infinite divisibility of geometric space, inadmissible for the chevalier de Méré; today it would be general relativity or Schrödinger's cat, at once dead and alive.

In a first fragment, Pascal contrasts the intuitive mind and the geometrical mind. Both are scientific, but they stem from different orders: one property of the intuitive approach is that it excels at "drawing consequences from a small number of principles," at "penetrating the consequences of principles vividly and profoundly"; the geometrical approach, for its part, excels at "drawing the consequences of things where there are many principles" and is able to "understand a great number of principles without confusing them." Or, in another formulation: "One is strength and rectitude of the mind, the other is amplitude of the mind" (669).

For the intuitive approach, Pascal gives the example of the "effects of water," referring to his own work on the weight of air and the void. The distinction is the one between physics and geometry, areas that exercise one's mind differently, as Pascal knew from experience.

In a second fragment, Pascal opposes the geometrical mind, with its "principles that are palpable but remote from common usage," to the mind steered by finesse, also an intuitive approach but one whose "principles are in common usage and visible to everyone" yet "so disconnected and in such great numbers that it is almost impossible that some aren't missed" (670).

We need to avoid yet another misunderstanding: it is always a matter of positing principles and deducing consequences from them. The intuitive mind thus cannot be confused with the heart, which for Pascal is the instinct of first principles (time, space, numbers). What Pascal is saying is that for those two types of minds, or three, the principles are not of the same order: for the intuitive mind, they are simple; for the geometrical mind, well-defined by numerous and unaccustomed; for the mind with finesse, familiar but numerous and delicate.

In this last case:

> We hardly see them, we feel them rather than see them, we go to infinite pains to make them felt by those who do not feel them on their own. These are such delicate things, and so numerous, that one needs a very delicate and very sharp sense for feeling them and judging them right and just according to that feeling, without being able, most often, to provide an orderly demonstration of the process, as in geometry, because one does not possess the principles, and because acquiring them would be an infinite undertaking. It is necessary to see the thing all at once in a single glance, and not by progressive reasoning, at least up to a certain point. (670)

The mind steered by finesse reasons "tacitly, naturally, and without art." As it is "accustomed to judging upon a single view"— thanks to its intuition—the steps in its reasoning are not explicit, but it is just as much a matter of reasoning as it is for the geometrical mind. Its principles stem from common usage, from the world; its domain is life, knowledge of humankind, knowledge that requires qualities different from those of physicists or geometricians. The mind steered by finesse is that of the moralist. "But," Pascal adds, "false minds are never either intuitive or geometrical" (670).

Pascal insists on the difference between minds. As the requisite qualities are different, "it is rare that geometricians are intuitive and that the intuitive are geometricians"; geometricians who want to deal with intuitive things make fools of themselves, while intuitive minds are deterred by the details in propositions made by geometricians, of which they understand nothing.

What Pascal does not say is that certain individuals possess both minds, that there are geometricians who are not only geometricians and intuitive minds that are not only intuitive; this was his own case, and it made him a prince of the mind, as lucid in the sciences as in morality.

40

"L'honnête Homme"

Pascal had the feeling that he lacked finesse in comparison to his worldly friends. The chevalier of Méré wrote to him in 1653 that he was resisting his friend's "long arguments drawn out from line to line," and he claimed to have "disabused" him (*OC* 3:353). Pascal's friends defended a different style in the search for truth, which inspired his conceptions of the heart and finesse.

Writing to tell Fermat that he would have to give up a planned visit in August 1660 because of his health, Pascal added:

> Although you are the one in all of Europe whom I take to be the greatest geometrician, it would not be that quality that would have drawn me; but I picture so much intelligence and *honnêteté* in your conversation, that I would have sought you out for that reason. For to speak frankly with you of geometry, I find it the highest exercise of the mind; but at the same time, I know it to be so futile

that I see little difference between a mere geometrician and a skillful artisan. (*OC* 4:923)

At the end of his life, Pascal considered *honnêteté* and conversation superior to science. One fragment in the *Pensées* recalls his evolution:

> I had spent a long time studying the abstract sciences, and the little communication that can emerge from them had discouraged me. When I began to study mankind, I saw that those abstract sciences were not appropriate for man, and that I was straying more from my condition by delving into them than others do by remaining unacquainted with them. But I believed I had found at least a number of companions in the study of man, and that that was the real study appropriate for man. I was wrong: there are even fewer who study man than who study geometry. (566)

Seeking knowledge of humankind, Pascal found no predecessors, and here, too, he had to invent his own method.

The honnête homme is first of all someone who is honorable, sociable, courteous, and polite. But Pascal's friends had a more elevated conception of *honnêteté*. For them, it was moral beauty that insisted on seeking the happiness of all, on seeking peace, "which is the sovereign good" (116). "All men seek to be happy" (181); this is the premise common to *honnêteté* and the *Pensées*. *Honnêteté* is thus the art of pleasing, of making oneself agreeable to all, of making oneself loved, an art of living in society that, according to Pascal's friends Méré and Mitton, both theoreticians of *honnêteté*, includes the happiness of others, altruism: "*Honnêteté* must . . . be considered the desire to be happy, but in such a way that makes others happy too," according to Mitton ("Pensées sur l'honnêteté" ["Thoughts on honesty"]). The moral virtues are for them inseparable from their social value:

> To make oneself happy, with less difficulty, and to be so assuredly, without fear of being troubled in one's happiness, we must act in such a way that others are happy with us: for if we claim to think solely about ourselves, we find continual opposition, and when we want to be happy only on condition that others are happy simultaneously, all the obstacles are lifted, and everyone lends us a hand. It is this moderation consisting of happiness for ourselves and for others that we must call *honnêteté*, which is nothing, if well understood, but well-governed self-love. (" Pensées sur l'honnêteté")

After his conversion, Pascal distanced himself from his friends, but there remains something of the ideal of *honnêteté* in the *Pensées*. The honnête homme is, as Montaigne would have it, universal, average, simply human:

> One must not be able [to say] about him that he is a mathematician, or a preacher, or eloquent, but rather that he is an *honnête homme*. This universal quality alone pleases me. When upon seeing a man one remembers his book, that is a bad sign. I would prefer that one notice no quality except by encountering it and having the opportunity to benefit from it, NE QUID NIMIS [nothing to excess], for fear that one quality should take over and be permanently associated with the person. (532)

Pascal denounces the pedantry of specialists and the narrowness of geometricians and poets on the same basis as that of the embroiderer:

> One is not recognized in this world as someone who knows about verse if one hasn't put up the sign of a poet, a mathematician, etc. But universal people do not want a sign and barely differentiate between the trade of a poet and that of an embroiderer. (486)

Ideally, the honnête homme, the universal man, ought to know everything. Lacking that, he should situate himself in the middle, in mediocrity:

> Since one cannot be universal by knowing everything that can be known about everything, one must know a little about everything. For it is much finer to know something about everything than to know everything about one thing. This universality is the most beautiful. If one could have both, all the better. But if one has to choose, one must choose the second. (228)

Finally, *honnêteté* is the condition for friendship, again as for Montaigne: "(*I hate the buffoon and the stuffed shirt equally.*) One would make a friend of neither. . . . The rule is *honnêteté*. / Poet and not *honnête homme*" (503).

41

M. de Mons, Louis de Montalte, Amos Dettonville, Salomon de Tultie

"May God never abandon me!" (*OC* 1:602): these were Pascal's last words. In the "Memorial," despite the confidence and certainty expressed, Pascal also asked: "My God, will you abandon me?" (742). Doubt is inseparable from faith. That is why the anguish that the *Pensées* seeks to induce in the libertine is not a foreign feeling to their author.

A number of fragments in the *Pensées* are tragic, austere, pious, and / or edifying, but others, or even the same ones, are full of verve, funny, mocking, or facetious: "Men are so necessarily mad that it would be mad by another twist of madness not to be mad" (31).

Pascal was something of a jouster and a game player. He liked masks, doubles, pseudonyms. In the midst of the campaign he was waging in the *Provincial Letters* against the learned doctors and the Jesuits in 1656, he hid out in the Roi David inn near the

Sorbonne, across from the Collège de Clermont (the future Lycée Louis-le-Grand and a Jesuit stronghold), under the name M. de Mons, borrowed from his paternal grandmother.

The rebellious streak, the amusing tone of the political pamphlets known as Mazarinades, along with their jubilant ferocity, ensured the success of the "little letters" in Paris salons among the men of the world and some women. Pascal got caught up in the game, taking pleasure in clandestinity and mocking banter, having fun continuing the series. The applause made Mother Angélique uncomfortable; she disapproved of the suspicious glory and the worldly vanity won by an "eloquence that amuses more people than it converts."[1] The *Provincial Letters* were published without an author's name, but when they were collected in early 1657, they were attributed to Louis de Montalte, one of Pascal's pseudonyms.

When he started the contest of the wheel, or the cycloid, in 1658, the challenge posed to European mathematicians was anonymous. But when he brought together his texts on the cycloid, still under the spell of clandestinity, he did so in the *Letters to A. Dettonville,* an anagram of Louis de Montalte (December 1658– February 1659).

We have to imagine a teasing Pascal, joking with the duc de Roannez, Méré, or Mitton. In every mathematician, there is a mischievous schoolboy: "We don't imagine Plato and Aristotle except draped in long robes. These were honnêtes hommes, laughing with

---

1. Mère Angélique, in a letter to Antoine Le Maistre dated April 2, 1656, following Pascal's fifth *Provincial Letter.*

their friends. And when they amused themselves by producing their *Laws* and their *Polemics,* it was as if to make rules for an asylum of madmen" (457).

Horror reigns in the *Pensées,* but there is also savor, succulence:

> The writing style of Epictetus, Montaigne, and Salomon de Tultie
> is the most common, the most suggestive, the kind that stays with
> us longer and is most often cited, because it is composed entirely
> of thoughts born of life's ordinary conversations. (618)

The mottos of Salomon de Tultie, another anagram of Louis de Montalte and Amos Dettonville, grew out of familiar conversation, like those of Epictetus and Montaigne. The intuitive mind reasons according to ordinary principles, and "nothing is more common than good things" (*OC* 3:427). The *Pensées* do not hesitate to gather amusing examples, like Cleopatra's nose or Cromwell's bladder, and curious observations: "Why is it that a limping man doesn't annoy us but a lame mind does?" (132). Or: "Two similar faces, neither of which makes us laugh by itself, together induce laughter by their resemblance" (47).

Yes, we live in terror, and life is unjust:

> Let us imagine a number of men in chains, all sentenced to death,
> some of whom have their throats slit every day while the others
> look on; those who remain see their own condition in that of their
> fellows, and, looking at each other in pain and despair, await
> their turn. (686)

Malraux must have remembered this in *The Human Condition* and Camus in *The Plague.*

But Pascal never took himself too seriously:

> Let no one say that I had nothing new to say: the arrangement of
> the material is new. In a game of handball, both players hit the
> same ball, but one places it better. (575)

Let us end with this light, ironic image of Pascal's writing and life
as a game. May it never abandon us!

Works Cited

WORKS BY BLAISE PASCAL

Les Pensées de Pascal. Edited by Jean Mesnard. Paris: SEDES-CDU, 1993.

Les Provinciales, Pensées, et opuscules divers. Edited by Philippe Sellier and Gérard Ferreyrolles. Paris: Librairie Générale française, 2004.

OC (Œuvres complètes). 4 vols. Edited by Jean Mesnard. Paris: Desclée de Brouwer, 1991 (vols. 1–2), 1992 (vols. 3–4).

PL (Pascal: The Provincial Letters). Translated by A. J. Krailsheimer. London: Penguin Books, 1967. First published 1657.

"De l'art de persuader." *OC* 3:413–428.

"Discours sur la condition des grands." *OC* 4:1028–1034.

"Écrit sur la conversion du pêcheur." *OC* 4:35–44.

"Écrits sur la grâce." *OC* 3:487–799.

"Entretien avec Monsieur de Sacy sur Épictète et Montaigne." *OC* 3:76–157.

"Le mémorial." *OC* 3:19–56.

"Lettre à la Sérénissime Reine de Suède." *OC* 2:923–926.

"Lettre de Monsieur Pascal à Monsieur de Fermat." *OC* 4:922–923.

"Lettres à Mademoiselle de Roannez." *OC* 3:996–1047.

"Lettres de A. Dettonville." *OC* 4:407–566.

"Prière pour demander à Dieu le bon usage des maladies." *OC* 4:964–1012.

"Récit de la grande expérience de l'équilibre des liqueurs." *OC* 2:653–690.

"Traité du triangle arithmétique." *OC* 2:1173–1332.

WORKS BY OTHER AUTHORS

Arnauld, (Mère) Angélique. "Lettre à Antoine Le Maistre." In Pascal, *Les Provinciales, Pensées, et opuscules divers,* April 2, 1656, p. 195.

Augustine. *Concerning the City of God against the Pagans.* Translated by Henry Bettenson. London: Penguin, 1984. Composed 413–426.

Augustine. *Confessions.* Translated by Thomas Williams. Indianapolis: Hackett, 2019. Composed 397–400.

Augustine. *On the Trinity.* Bks. 8–15. Translated by Stephen McKenna. Cambridge: Cambridge University Press, 2002. Composed c. 417.

Bernard of Clairvaux. "Treatise on the Love of God." In *Select Treatises of S. Bernard of Clairvaux: De diligendo Deo,* edited by Watkin W. Williams, pp. 8–69. Cambridge: Cambridge University Press, 1926.

Chateaubriand, François-René de. *The Genius of Christianity; or, The Spirit and Beauty of the Christian Religion: By Viscount de Chateaubriand.* Edited and translated by Charles I. White. Baltimore: John Murphy; Philadelphia: J. B. Lippincott, 1856.

Descartes, René. *Meditations on First Philosophy.* Translated by John Cottingham. Cambridge: Cambridge University Press, 2013. First published 1641.

Descotes, Dominique. *Pascal, auteur spirituel.* Paris: Champion, 2006.

Goldmann, Lucien. *The Hidden God: A Study of Tragic Vision in the Pensées of Pascal and the Tragedies of Racine.* Translated by Philip Thody. New York: Humanities Press, 1964. First published 1955.

Green, Julien. *Journal.* In Vol. 4, *Œuvres complètes.* Paris: Bibliothèque de la Pléiade, 1976.

La Bruyère, Jean de. *Les caractères, ou les moeurs de ce siècle.* Edited by G. Servois and A. Rébelliau. 3rd ed. Paris: Hachette, 1894. First published 1687.

Mitton, Damien. "Pensées sur l'honnêteté." In *Œuvres mêlées,* by Charles de Saint-Évremond, pt. 6. Paris: Claude Barbin, 1680.

Montaigne, Michel de. *The Complete Works: Essays, Travel Journals, Letters.* Translated by Donald M. Frame. New York: Penguin Books, 2003. First published 1580.

Pascal, Jacqueline. "Lettres de Jacqueline Pascal sur la conversion de son frère." In Pascal, *OC* 3:61–69.

Périer, Gilberte. "La vie de Jacqueline Pascal." In Pascal, *OC* 1:652–671.

Périer, Gilberte. "La vie de Monsieur Pascal." In Pascal, *OC* 1:572–602 (1st version), 1:603–642 (2nd version).

Périer, Marguerite. "Mémoire sur Pascal et sa famille." In Pascal, *OC* 1:1091–1105.

Proust, Marcel. *The Way by Swann's.* Translated by Lydia Davis. Vol. 1, *In Search of Lost Time.* New York: Penguin Books, 2003. First published 1913.

Proust, Marcel. *Finding Time Again.* Translated by Ian Patterson. Vol. 7, *In Search of Lost Time.* New York: Penguin Books, 2023. First published 1927.

Sainte-Beuve, Charles-Augustin. *Port-Royal.* Paris: Gallimard, 1951–1953. First published 1848.

Sarraute, Nathalie. *Paul Valéry et l'Enfant d'Éléphant: Flaubert le précurseur.*
    Paris: Gallimard, 1986.

Valéry, Paul. "Variations on a 'Pensée.'" *Collected Works of Paul Valéry*, vol. 9,
    pp. 86–107. Princeton, NJ: Princeton University Press, 1956–1975.

Voltaire, François-Marie Arouet. "Lettre à Condorcet, 7 septembre
    1776." In *Condorcet, Arithmétique politique: Textes rares ou inédits
    (1767–1789),* edited by Bernard Bru and Pierre Crépel, p. 115. Paris:
    Presses Universitaires de France, 1994.

Voltaire, François-Marie Arouet. "Lettre à M. de's Gravesande." In
    Œuvres complètes de Voltaire. Vol. 36, *Correspondance,* p. 63. Paris:
    Garnier, 1880.

Voltaire, François-Marie Arouet. *Philosophical Letters; Or, Letters Regarding
    the English Nation..* Translated by Prudence L. Steiner. Indianapolis:
    Hackett, 2007. First published 1733.